SCHOOL LIBRARY MEDIA SERIES

Edited by Diane de Cordova Biesel

1. *Chalk Talk Stories*, written and illustrated by Arden Druce, 1993.
2. *Toddler Storytime Programs*, by Diane Briggs, 1993.
3. *Alphabet: A Handbook of ABC Books and Book Extensions for the Elementary Classroom*, second edition, by Patricia L. Roberts, 1994.
4. *Cultural Cobblestones: Teaching Cultural Diversity*, by Lynda Miller, Theresa Steinlage, and Mike Printz, 1994.
5. *ABC Books and Activities: From Preschool to High School*, by Cathie Hilterbran Cooper, 1996.
6. *ZOOLUTIONS: A Mathematical Expedition with Topics for Grades 4 through 8*, by Anne Burgunder and Vaunda Nelson, 1996.
7. *Library Lessons for Grades 7–9*, by Arden Druce, 1997.
8. *Counting Your Way through 1–2–3 Books and Activities*, by Cathie Hilterbran Cooper, 1997.
9. *Art and Children: Using Literature to Expand Creativity*, by Robin W. Davis, 1996.
10. *Story Programs: A Source Book of Materials*, second edition, by Carolyn Sue Peterson and Ann Fenton, 1998.
11. *Taking Humor Seriously in Children's Literature: Literature-Based Mini-Units and Humorous Books for Children Ages 5–12*, by Patricia L. Roberts, 1997.
12. *Multicultural Friendship Stories and Activities for Children, Ages 5–14*, by Patricia L. Roberts, 1997.
13. *Side by Side: Twelve Multicultural Puppet Plays*, by Jean M. Pollock, 1997.
14. *Reading Fun: Quick and Easy Activities for the School Library Media Center*, by Mona Kerby, 1997.
15. *Paper Bag Puppets*, by Arden Druce with illustrations by Geraldine Hulbert, Cynthia Johnson, Harvey H. Lively, and Carol Ditter Waters, 1998.
16. *Once Upon a Childhood: Fingerplays, Action Rhymes, and Fun Times for the Very Young*, Dolores C. Chupela, 1998.
17. *Bulletin Bored? or Bulletin Boards!: (K–12)*, Patricia Sivak and Mary Anne Passatore, 1998.

Once Upon a Childhood

*Fingerplays, Action Rhymes, and
Fun Times for the Very Young*

Dolores C. Chupela

School Library Media Series, No. 16

The Scarecrow Press, Inc.
Lanham, Md., & London
1998

SCARECROW PRESS, INC.

Published in the United States of America
by Scarecrow Press, Inc.
4720 Boston Way
Lanham, Maryland 20706

4 Pleydell Gardens
Kent CT20 2DN, England

British Library Cataloguing in Publication Information Available

Library of Congress Cataloging-in-Publication Data

Chupela, Dolores, 1952–
    Once upon a childhood : fingerplays, action rhymes, and fun times
for the very young / Dolores C. Chupela.
        p. cm. — (School library media series ; no. 16)
    Includes bibliographical references and index.
    ISBN 0-8108-3485-5 (pbk. : alk. paper)
      1. Children's libraries—Activity programs—United States.
  2. Finger play—United States.   3. Children's poetry, American.
  4. Games—United States. I. Title. II. Series.
Z675.S3C4979   1998
027.62'5—dc21   98-3301
                                                CIP

∞™ The paper used in this publication meets the minimum requirements
of American National Standard for Information Sciences—Permanence of
Paper for Printed Library Materials, ANSI Z39.48–1984. Manufactured in the
United States of America.

In memory of:

My godfather, Joseph Pazdon Sr.
(you are truly an angel among us)

In honor of:

My parents, John and Cecilia Chupela, the two heroes in my life who never discouraged me from dreaming impossible dreams and making them come true. Love you!

With special thanks to:

Mary Ann Peterson and the New Jersey Association of Kindergarten Educators for "adopting" me as one of your own. You are all an inspiration.

My extended family of aunts, uncles, cousins, and friends; you are all so beautiful in my eyes.

Lastly, to country musicians everywhere: Your wonderful songs have made my fingers "line dance" over the keys as I wrote this book! Love y'all!

Contents

Editor's Foreword

The School Library Media Series is directed to the school library media specialist, particularly the building-level librarian. The multifaceted role of the librarian as educator, collection developer, curriculum developer, and information specialist is examined. The series includes concise, practical books on topical and current subjects related to programs and services.

In *Once Upon a Childhood: Fingerplays, Action Rhymes, and Fun Times for the Very Young*, Dolores Chupela has devised original rhymes about animals, objects, and themes followed by ideas for related activities, crafts, and stories. These have been arranged in alphabetical order from "Alligators" to "Worms." Don't you know a child who would like to wiggle like a worm or visit a turkey farmer?

The author has provided an extensive list of other books of fingerplays, as well as a bibliography of recommended books for young children. This book will be helpful to the librarian, the teacher, or the parent.

Series Editor
Diane de Cordova Biesel

Introduction

Fingerplays and action rhymes have been important parts of a youngster's childhood for generations simply because children truly enjoy them.

I, for one, can still remember the joy and sense of accomplishment that I felt as a child when I recited "The Eentsy Weentsy Spider" for the very first time! I just couldn't wait for the sun to come out and dry up all the rain!

This began a lifelong love of fingerplays and action rhymes—so much so that I can still feel a similar sense of joy and accomplishment when I write and teach my very own rhymes to the children who attend my library programs.

Besides being fun, fingerplays and action rhymes are easy for children to learn and remember. They are perfect for participation and help to introduce little ones to the world around them.

Once learned, a child can recite, as well as perform, the accompanying actions alone. Or the rhymes can be used to provide warm and nurturing interaction between adult and child.

Fingerplays and action rhymes help a youngster develop motor and language skills. They also help to "plant the seeds" for the enjoyment and appreciation of poetry in later years. The rhymes are excellent additions to a program presentation or a story-time session. They can be used as an introduction to a special classroom theme or topic, and they can also be expanded to include stick puppets, flannelboard stories, songs, games, and simple crafts.

Fingerplays and action rhymes make a wonderful "take-home" activity for both the adult and the child. They can serve to extend and reinforce a positive library or classroom experience.

The purpose of this book is to provide librarians, teachers, programmers, child-care providers, and anyone who spends time with young children access to original fingerplays and action rhymes on a wide variety of topics that are familiar to little children. Accompanying the fingerplays and action rhymes are suggested stories for reading and sharing, along with an assortment of related activities such as flannelboard ideas, simple crafts, and puppetry suggestions, as well as program and presentation tips.

As you use the activities and make new friends with the characters on the following pages, may you, too, feel the same joie de vivre that I did when being introduced to the Eentsy Weentsy Spider once upon a childhood. Have fun!

Using Fingerplays and Action Rhymes

Fingerplays and action rhymes add movement to a program or presentation. They offer the participants a change of pace.

Children are afforded the opportunity to become actively involved in the program or presentation, which is an important factor in maintaining a child's attention.

Fingerplays and action rhymes are excellent resources that can be used to ease the way into a quiet listening time. They can help to get the "wiggles" out!

When using fingerplays and action rhymes, choose those that are simple enough for your audience to handle. As the little ones become familiar with them, proceed to others that are more challenging.

Practice ahead of time before presenting.

Some children may be hesitant to participate. Don't become unnerved by this; when they witness all of the fun, they will soon want to jump in!

When teaching fingerplays and action rhymes, do so for short periods of time. This will give the child pleasure in learning and eliminate boredom.

Repetition helps children learn, so repeat them often. Encourage children's creativity by allowing them to create their own rhymes and accompanying motions.

Fingerplays and action rhymes are a wonderful shared learning experience that is rewarding for both adult and child.

So, as you use the following fingerplays and action rhymes, I sincerely hope that you will have as much fun presenting them as I did in creating them!

Fingerplays/Action Rhymes and Accompanying Activities

The following section contains over fifty original fingerplays/action rhymes based on a wide variety of topics that are arranged alphabetically beginning with *A* for "Alligators" to *W* for "Worms"!

Each fingerplay/action rhyme topic also contains stories for reading and sharing, craft activities that utilize an assortment of common everyday items, creative movement, bulletin board and room decoration ideas, games, musical activities, and contests.

Parental involvement is emphasized, and community outreach is stressed.

Last, but not least, the use of imagination is highly encouraged!

So get those fingers moving, those toes tapping; sprinkle some pixie dust, add a moonbeam or two, and reach for the stars!

Alligators

FINGERPLAY/ACTION RHYME

Alligators

Alligators swimming in my soup,
(pretend to swim)
Alligators doing the loop-the-loop,
(hold arms out to side, spin)

Alligators in my hair,
(ruffle hair)
Alligators without a care!
(smile)

Alligators in the sun,
(point to sky)
Alligators having loads of fun!
(giggle)

Alligators in a balloon,
(point to sky)
Alligators flying to the moon!
(jump in air)

Bye!

STORIES TO READ AND SHARE

Brown, Ruth. *Crazy Charlie*

DeGroat, Diane. *Alligator's Toothache*

Hurd, Thatcher. *Mama Don't Allow*

Mayer, Mercer. *There's an Alligator Under My Bed*

Stone, Kazuko G. *Aligay Saves the Day*

Stone, Kazuko G. *Good Night Twinklegator*

Alligators

CRAFT

Balloon Gator

Supplies

Long green balloon
Green construction paper
Tape
Magic Marker

Blow up long green balloon. Draw and cut out paper feet. Tape in place. Draw "skin" with Magic Marker. Cut an oblong piece of construction paper (two pieces). Tape on the front of balloon to form mouth. Draw eyes and teeth with Magic Marker.

ACTIVITIES

- Research the differences between alligators and crocodiles. Find out where they live, what they eat, and so on.

- Slither and slink like a gator!

- Write a lo-o-o-ong alligator tale.

- Write alligator jokes and riddles.

- Use an alligator puppet to demonstrate toothbrushing!

- Using a projector, make shadow gators with hands by placing palms together and opening and closing them.

Ants

FINGERPLAY/ACTION RHYME

Ants in the Kitchen

Ants in the kitchen eating their lunch,
(pretend to eat)
Ants in the kitchen go munch-munch.
("munch")

No more cheese, no more bread,
(shake head)
Why don't you eat the peas instead?
(make little circles with index finger and
    thumb)

Ants

Ants on pants,
(touch leg, pants)
Ants from France,
(point right)

Ants on the table,
(point down)
Ants on Aunt Mabel!
(point to someone)

Oh me, oh my, ants wave bye, bye!
(wave)

STORIES TO READ AND SHARE

Allison, Beverley. *Effie*

Demuth, Patricia Brennan. *Those Amazing Ants*

Dorros, Arthur. *Ant Cities*

Freschet, Berniece. *The Ants Go Marching*

Jackson, Ellen. *Ants Can't Dance*

Pinczes, Elinor J. *One Hundred Hungry Ants*

Ants

CRAFT

Ant Feeler Headband

Supplies

Red, brown, or black construction paper
Stapler or tape

To make headband, cut a strip of construction paper long enough to fit comfortably around a child's head. Staple or tape ends together. Cut two smaller strips of construction paper for feelers. Staple or tape to front of headband.

Ant City

Supplies

Brown construction paper
Black crayon or Magic Marker
Nontoxic glue
Black glitter

On brown construction paper, draw ant tunnels and rooms with crayon or Magic Marker. Add ants by coating paper lightly with nontoxic glue then sprinkling black glitter on glue to make ants.

ACTIVITIES

- Discuss different types of ants and how they live and grow.

- Buy an ant-farm kit for your program room or classroom, set up, and observe.

- Go on an "ant hunt" . . . look for different types of ants. Caution children against touching because some species bite.

- "Creep" through an ant tunnel.

- Put hand to head . . . wiggle "feelers"!

- Create an ant city on a bulletin board using construction paper and your imagination!

- Some ants like music, so create an ant song or invent an ant line dance! Perform wearing feelers (see *Craft*).

- For a special treat, serve a snack of "ant" pudding, yogurt, or ice cream sprinkled with chocolate "ant" jimmies!

- Write ant riddles and jokes; publish in a booklet titled "Ant-tics"!

Apples

FINGERPLAY/ACTION RHYME

Apple

An apple is delicious, round and red,
(make circle with arms)

An apple fell from the tree and bumped me on the head!
(make fist, tap head)

STORIES TO READ AND SHARE

Asch, Frank. *Oats and Wild Apples*

Gibbons, Gail. *The Seasons of Arnold's Apple Tree*

Hall, Zoe. *The Apple Pie Tree*

Orbach, Ruth. *Apple Pigs*

Apples

CRAFT

Apple Faces

Supplies

Red construction paper
Crayons
Magic Markers
Nontoxic paint

On red construction paper, draw an apple shape. With crayons, Magic Markers, or nontoxic paint, have children create their very own apple face. Provide examples such as a silly face, happy face, sad face, outrageous face, monster face, etc.

ACTIVITIES

- Obtain a variety of apples such as macintosh, golden delicious, macoon, or red delicious. Let children sample the different flavors. Vote for a favorite!

- Cut apart an apple and show the "star" inside (the seed area).

- Discuss how and where apples grow and their uses.

- Purchase apples and give one to each child to take home and share with someone special.

- Ask children to pretend that they are apples and "fall" gently from the tree!

- Create an apple bulletin board. Make a basket out of construction paper or poster board. Fill the basket with paper apples (one for each child). Print a child's name on each. Caption your bulletin board PICK OF THE CROP.

- Encourage children to munch an apple and "bite into a good book"! (See *Stories to Read and Share* for suggested titles.)

- Read the book *The Apple Pie Tree* and make an apple pie. The book contains an apple pie recipe.

Babies

FINGERPLAY/ACTION RHYME

Little Baby Sister

Little baby sister sitting on my lap,
(pat lap)
Little baby sister, it's time for a nap.
(pretend to sleep)

I'll read you a story and sing you a song,
(pretend to read and sing)
And sweet, sweet dreams will soon come
    along.
(fall asleep)

Baby Brother

I have a baby brother for all the world to see,
I have a baby brother who looks a lot like me.
(point to yourself)

His eyes are green and his hair is brown,
(point to eyes, touch hair)
He can make me smile and he can make me
    frown.
(smile, frown)

I love my baby brother, oh yes I do,
Our favorite game is peekaboo!
(put hands over face, "peek" out)

STORIES TO READ AND SHARE

Armstrong, Jennifer. *That Terrible Baby*

Chocolate, Debbi. *On the Day I Was Born*

Gliori, Debi. *Mr. Bear Babysits*

Gliori, Debi. *My Little Brother*

Gliori, Debi. *New Big Sister*

Keller, Holly. *Geraldine's Baby Brother*

Kopper, Lisa. *Daisy Thinks She Is a Baby*

Levinson, Riki. *Me Baby!*

Polushkin, Maria. *Baby Brother Blues*

Shute, Linda. *How I Named the Baby*

Babies

CRAFT

Baby-Food Jar Paperweight

Supplies

Small baby-food jar
One of the following: Colored sand
                        Marbles
                        Aquarium gravel
                        Seashells
                        Any items you want to put inside!

Remove the manufacturer's label from a small baby-food jar. Make sure that the jar has been washed out and dried thoroughly. Fill the jar with any of the above items. Screw lid on to jar securely. Turn upside down to create paperweight.

ACTIVITIES

- Decorate your program area or classroom with balloons and streamers. Hold a "Family Day" celebration. Invite family members to your celebration for stories, games, and refreshments.

- Have children bring in baby pictures of themselves along with a current photo. Display on a bulletin board with the caption LOOK HOW WE'VE GROWN. Put the photos on paper flowers (the baby picture on a bud, the current photo on a fully opened blossom).

- Have children make baby-food jar paperweights (see *Craft*). Wrap up and give as gifts to family members who attend your celebration.

- Encourage children to write and illustrate stories about their family members.

- Collect baby products for those in your town who are in need. Take to homeless shelters, social service agencies, and so forth.

Bees

FINGERPLAY/ACTION RHYME

Baby Bumblebee

Buz-z-zing baby bumblebee,
Buz-z-zing by me,
(point to yourself)

Buz-z-zing by a ladybug,
Buz-z-zing by a flea.
(flap wings)

Lookin' for a daisy,
Lookin' for a rose,
(pretend to search, put hand on forehead)

Don't you dare buz-z-z the tip of my nose!
(shake head, touch nose)

Fuzzy Buzzy Bumblebee

Fuzzy Buzzy Bumblebee all black and yellow,
Fuzzy Buzzy Bumblebee, such a tiny little
    fellow.
(indicate small with thumb and forefinger)

Watch as he flies from flower to flower,
("fly," flap wings)
Hide, Fuzzy Buzzy, it's starting to shower!
(hide, make rain by fluttering fingers)

STORIES TO READ AND SHARE

Barton, Byron. *Buzz, Buzz, Buzz*

Carle, Eric. *The Honeybee and the Robber*

Ernst, Lisa Campbell. *A Colorful Adventure of the Bee Who Left Home One Monday Morning and What He Found along the Way*

Lobel, Arnold. *The Rose in My Garden*

Polacco, Patricia. *The Bee Tree*

Wahl, Jan. *Follow Me, Cried Bee!*

West, Colin. *"Buzz, Buzz, Buzz," Went Bumble Bee*

Bees

CRAFT

Balloon Bees

Supplies

Yellow round balloons
Black Magic Marker
Optional: Balloon clip

Blow up yellow balloons and knot or clip shut with balloon clip. Make bee "stripes" with black Magic Marker around body of balloon. Draw eyes. "Fly" bee by gently tapping it into the air.

ACTIVITIES

- Host a "Buzzing Bee": See who can make the loudest buzz, the most quiet, the most unusual, the silliest, the longest, etc.

- Designate a "Bee Day"; dress in yellow and black!

- Invite a beekeeper to visit.

- Eat something yummy made with honey!

- Discuss bees and their characteristics.

- Explain what measures to take if one encounters a bee; include first aid procedures.

- Using balloon bees (see *Craft*), have a "bee race" by flying the bee to the hive (hive can be a bag, box, etc.).

- Ask the children to identify words that begin with the letter *B*.

Bread

FINGERPLAY/ACTION RHYME

Mom Bakes Bread

Mom bakes bread, yes she does,
Mom bakes bread just because.
(nod head)

She rolls it, kneads it, and bakes it just right,
(roll bread, knead bread)
Oh what a treat on Saturday night!
(rub tummy, smack lips)

Bread

Roll the dough, knead it just so,
(roll, knead)
Let it rise, nice and slow.
(raise hands in the air)

Put it in the oven, watch it bake,
(peek into oven)
I wonder how long it will take?
(shrug shoulders)

STORIES TO READ AND SHARE

DePaola, Tomie. *Tony's Bread*

Johnson, Hannah Lyons. *Let's Bake Bread*

Lindsey, Treska. *When Batistine Made Bread*

Morris, Ann. *Bread Bread Bread*

Bread

CRAFT

Clay Bread

Supplies

Soft clay

Using soft clay as your "dough," knead and roll "bread." Shape into loaves, rolls, pastry, pretzels, braided bread, etc. Let harden.

ACTIVITIES

- Bake bread from scratch or from prepared dough. Bake a roll for each child. Explain how and why bread dough rises. Bake extra and take to your local food bank.

- Visit a bakery or have a baker visit you.

- Sample different types of bread such as white, rye, whole wheat, pita, bagels, raisin, pumpernickel, soft pretzels, etc. Feed leftovers to the birds!

- Ask each child to bring in a small loaf of bread and donate to local food bank.

- Make toast.

- Invite a child's family member to visit and bake bread. (Ethnic specialties will demonstrate the wide variety of bread around the world.)

- Use the book *Bread Bread Bread* (see *Stories to Read and Share*) to learn about breads around the world.

- Read the book *Let's Bake Bread* (see *Stories to Read and Share*), which has a simple bread recipe and explains how bread bakes.

 # Butterflies

PRETTY ORANGE BUTTERFLY

Pretty orange butterfly, flap your wings,
(flap arms)
Soar to where the sparrow sings,
(spread arms)
Pretty orange butterfly sitting in the tree,
(point up)
Pretty orange butterfly, what do you see?
(pretend to look around)

STORIES TO READ AND SHARE

Cassie, Brian, and Jerry Pallotta. *The Butterfly Alphabet Book*

Gibbons, Gail. *Monarch Butterfly*

Heiligman, Deborah. *From Caterpillar to Butterfly*

Taylor, Kim. *Butterfly*

Butterflies

CRAFT

Butterfly Tree

Supplies

Construction paper
Green tissue paper
Pictures of butterflies cut out of magazines or butterfly stickers
Glue

Using construction paper, cut out the outline of a tree trunk and its branches. Glue on to a contrasting piece of construction paper. Add "leaves" by tearing small pieces of green tissue paper and gluing them to the tree branches. Cut out pictures of butterflies (or use butterfly stickers) and adhere to tree.

ACTIVITIES

- Flap arms as if they were butterfly wings.
- Invite a butterfly expert to visit with the children, or visit a butterfly farm.
- Purchase a caterpillar kit and raise your own butterflies. Release your butterflies after they have hatched. Remember, they are not pets.
- Make butterflies from tissue paper, and decorate program area or classroom.
- Discuss butterfly migration.
- Go on a "butterfly hunt": Look around outside and see how many can be found.
- Encourage children to create their very own unique butterfly using crayons, Magic Markers, and other assorted items. Give each butterfly a name, and display.
- Make butterfly "shadows": Using a light projector, focus on a light-colored wall. Cross arms at wrists and flap hands to make shadow butterflies.

Camels

FINGERPLAY/ACTION RHYME

Camel

A camel has humps,
(bend over)

And a camel has bumps.
(make "waves" with hands)

Have you ever seen a camel with the mumps?

I haven't, have you?
(shake head)

STORIES TO READ AND SHARE

Goodenow, Earle. *The Last Camel*

Hamsa, Bobbie. *Your Pet Camel*

Pete, Bill. *Pamela Camel*

Roberts, Bethany, and Patricia Hubbell. *Camel Caravan*

Wells, Rosemary. *Abul*

Camels

CRAFT

Sandpaper Desert

Supplies

Small squares of sandpaper
Crayons

Give each child a small piece of sandpaper. Draw a desert scene on it with crayons.

OPTIONAL: "Print" your desert scene on to white paper by placing sandpaper facedown on paper. Iron the back with hot iron. (This should be done only under adult supervision.)

ACTIVITIES

- Walk like a camel!
- Learn about these "ships of the desert," such as their capacity to hold water in their humps.
- Take an imaginary trip through the desert . . . what do you see?
- Take a trip to the zoo and visit with a camel up close and personal!
- Design a desert scene for program area or classroom.
- Have a "sand corner" in program area or classroom for children to play in.

Cars and Trucks

FINGERPLAY/ACTION RHYME

Little Red Car

Little red car riding down the street,
(drive)
Little red car, you sure look neat!
(continue to drive)

Big shiny wheels, a horn that goes beep,
(beep-beep)
When I grow up, you'll be mine to keep.
(stand on toes)

Big Blue Truck

Big blue truck heading down the road,
(drive)
Big blue truck carrying a heavy load.
(continue to drive)

Traveling near, traveling far,
(point right, point left)
I wave to the driver from the seat of my car!
(wave)

STORIES TO READ AND SHARE

Crews, Donald. *Truck*

Demarest, Chris L. *My Little Red Car*

Gibbons, Gail. *Trucks*

Kulman, Andrew. *Red Light Stop, Green Light Go*

Newton, Laura P. *William the Vehicle King*

Royston, Angela. *Cars*

Sutherland, Harry A. *Dad's Car Wash*

Cars and Trucks

CRAFT

Construction Paper Traffic Light

Supplies

Black, red, green, and yellow construction paper
Scissors
Glue

Trace circles of the same size on the red, green, and yellow construction paper, then cut out circles. Make sure that they are small enough to fit on black sheet of construction paper. Glue circles in appropriate places on black construction paper to make traffic light.

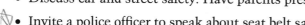

ACTIVITIES

- "Toot" horn, "drive" truck and car, "wash" vehicles.
- Cut out pictures of cars and trucks. Design a city: Make roads, add cars and trucks, traffic signs, etc. Decorate program area or classroom.
- Tour a car/truck factory.
- Invite someone who specializes in antique vehicles to bring a vehicle to view.
- Discuss car and street safety. Have parents present.
- Invite a police officer to speak about seat belt safety. Invite drivers of various municipal vehicles to visit with their vehicles.
- Visit a car/truck repair shop. Have an auto mechanic speak to the children.
- Have someone donate small tires to make a tire park. Include parents in the project.
- Have a "tire roll." Conduct as if a relay race.
- Using little plastic or metal cars and trucks, have a mini car/truck race.

Caterpillars

FINGERPLAY/ACTION RHYME

Caterpillars

Caterpillars creep, caterpillars crawl,
(crawl)
Caterpillars can be big or they can be small.
(show "big," show "small")

Caterpillars tickle when they wiggle across my toes,
(wiggle toes)
Caterpillars, please don't sit upon my nose!
(point to nose)

Achoo!
(sneeze)

STORIES TO READ AND SHARE

Carle, Eric. *The Very Hungry Caterpillar*

Deluise, Dom. *Charlie the Caterpillar*

Heiligman, Deborah. *From Caterpillar to Butterfly*

Kent, Jack. *The Caterpillar and the Polliwog*

McBratney, Sam. *The Caterpillow Fight*

Caterpillars

CRAFT

Fuzzy Caterpillar

Supplies

Clip clothespin
Glue
Small pom-poms
Craft magnet
Wiggly eyes

To make caterpillar's body, glue small pom-poms on to the clothespin. Glue wiggly eyes on the "clip" end of the clothespin—this will be the caterpillar's head. Glue craft magnet on the underside of clothespin. Caterpillar can be attached to magnetic surface and can be used to hold children's artwork.

Sock Caterpillar

Supplies

Tube sock
Old pantyhose or craft fiberfill
Yarn or string
Fabric paint
Felt
Wiggly eyes
Glue

Stuff a tube sock with old pantyhose or craft fiberfill. At regularly spaced intervals, tie strips of yarn or string to form caterpillar's body. Trim yarn or string. Make eyes by painting with fabric paint or by gluing on wiggly eyes. Cut felt into circles and glue on body. Or give your caterpillar a "striped suit" by painting stripes with fabric paint.

ACTIVITIES

- Creep and crawl like a caterpillar; spin a chrysalis.

- Purchase a caterpillar kit and raise your own butterflies. Release your butterflies after they have hatched. Remember, they are not pets.

- Make a giant caterpillar for your program area or classroom by tracing large circles to form caterpillar's body. Decorate or have each child decorate a circle and add their name.

- Create a "caterpillar crawl" or "butterfly flutter" dance! Use colorful scarves as "wings." Put on soft music and let children flap scarves and "float" around the room or outside.

- Do caterpillar/butterfly face painting; check with parents beforehand. Take photos and display. Give photo to parents as a gift.

- Explain the metamorphosis of the caterpillar using the book *From Caterpillar to Butterfly* (see *Stories to Read and Share*) to aid in explaining the metamorphosis of the butterfly.

Chipmunks

FINGERPLAY/ACTION RHYME

Chester Chipmunk

Chester Chipmunk scurrying on the ground,
(make fingers run up arm)
Chester Chipmunk running all around.
(make fingers run up other arm)

Chester Chipmunk, so small and furry,
(make a tiny fist)
Chester Chipmunk found an acorn to bury!
(make digging motions with hands)

STORIES TO READ AND SHARE

Gruber, Suzanne. *Chatty Chipmunk's Nutty Day*

Haas, Jessie. *Chipmunk!*

Tunis, Edwin. *Chipmunks on the Doorstep*

Wolcott, Patty. *Beware of a Very Hungry Fox*

Chipmunks

CRAFT

Chipmunk Glove Puppet

Supplies

Garden glove
Black pom-poms
Brown pom-poms
Glue
Wiggly eyes

Glue black and brown pom-poms on each finger of the glove. Glue two wiggly eyes on each pom-pom. This will make five chipmunks to wiggle and jiggle!

ACTIVITIES

- "Bury" bags of peanuts: Ask children to pretend that they are chipmunks and "hunt" for the peanuts. This will be a fun way to provide a nutritious snack!

- If chipmunks reside in your area, try to observe their behavior; if not, look at pictures of them. The book *Chipmunks on the Doorstep* (see *Stories to Read and Share*) is a good source of information.

- Face paint chipmunk whiskers on children. Let them look in a mirror as they make "fat" cheeks!

- Make chipmunk stripes on children's backs by attaching a black streamer. Make a tail by tying brown and black streamers together.

- Get a pot of soil and bury an acorn. See if you can start an oak tree!

- Create chipmunk jokes and riddles; publish in a booklet titled "Chipmunk Chuckles"!

Clouds

FINGERPLAY/ACTION RHYME

Clouds

Clouds are fluffy and clouds are white,
(pretend to feel clouds)
Clouds can be seen both day and night.
(look up and cup hands over eyes)

They softly float up so high,
(pretend to float)
See the clouds in the deep blue sky.
(look and point up)

STORIES TO READ AND SHARE

DePaola, Tomie. *The Cloud Book*

Renberg, Dalia Hardof. *Hello, Clouds!*

Shaw, Charles G. *It Looked Like Spilt Milk*

Spier, Peter. *Dreams*

Clouds

CRAFT

Chalk Clouds

Supplies

Blue construction paper
White chalk
Facial tissue

Using blue construction paper to make "sky," give each child a piece of white chalk and ask them to draw cloud shapes. Smudge clouds with facial tissue for a muted, cloudy effect.

ACTIVITIES

- "Jump" and "roll" through clouds. "Float!"

- If weather permits, take children outside. Look for familiar shapes in the clouds. How many can you find?

- Invite a local meteorologist or science teacher to speak to the children about how clouds are formed. Learn the names of different types of clouds.

- Have a cloud-naming contest; award prizes for the silliest name, most original, most scientific, "cloudiest," etc.

Colors

FINGERPLAY/ACTION RHYME

Yellow

Yellow is the color of the sun in the sky,
(point up)
Yellow is the color of the bees buzzing by.
(make "buzz" sound)

Yellow is the color of the daffodil flowers,
(make a circle with hands to make daffodil)
Yellow is the color of my umbrella when it
    showers!
(make rain with fluttering fingers)

Green

Green bean, Green pea,
Green, green grass all around me!
(point to yourself)

Green car, going far,
(pretend to drive)
Green pickles in a jar!

Green crayon, green frog,
(croak!)
Green moss growing on a log!

Green fish, Green fish,
(swim)
Green spinach in a dish!

Yuck!
(make a face!)

Blue

Blue is the color of the jay in the tree,
(flap wings)
Blue is the color that looks best on me.
(point to yourself)

Blue is the color of my Daddy's eyes,
(point to eyes)
Blue is the color of the clear, clear skies.
(point up)

Red

Red is the color of the sweetest rose,
(pretend to smell)
Red is the color of my "winter" nose!
(point to nose)

Red kite in the summer sky,
(point up)
Red bird flying so high.
(flap wings)

Red is the color of my favorite ball,
(pretend to bounce a ball)
Red leaves on trees in the fall.
(make leaves by fluttering fingers)

STORIES TO READ AND SHARE

Baker, Alan. *White Rabbit's Color Book*

Ehlert, Lois. *Planting a Rainbow*

Hubbard, Patricia. *My Crayons Talk*

Kleven, Elisa. *The Lion and the Little Red Bird*

Kunhardt, Edith. *Red Day, Green Day*

Walsh, Ellen Stoll. *Mouse Paint*

Young, James. *A Million Chameleons*

Colors

CRAFT

Favorite Color Collage

Supplies

White paper
Glue
Ribbon
Crayons
Magic Markers
Glitter
Confetti
Chalk
Construction paper cut into bits
Miscellaneous colorful items

Give each child a piece of white paper. Ask each child his/her favorite color. Give each child an assortment of the above media in his/her favorite color. Create a color collage by applying glue to white paper and sprinkling the above items on the glue to create a design.

ACTIVITIES

- Read *Red Day, Green Day* (see *Stories to Read and Share*). Based upon the story, designate each day of the week as a different "Color Day." Wear the color designated on the appropriate day! After all of the colors are worn, have a "Rainbow Day." Serve rainbow sherbet and hand out rainbow lollipops. On "Rainbow Day," encourage each child to wear his/her favorite color. Take a photo of the group "rainbow"!

- Look through old magazines for items in the "color of the day." Cut out and display.

- Look through prism glasses for an "instant rainbow."

- Hang an old white sheet in your program area or classroom. Create an abstract mural of color by giving each child a color to paint. Display in a prominent area.

- Name the colors all around you.

Cookies

FINGERPLAY/ACTION RHYME

Cookies

Cookies so tasty, cookies so yummy,
(rub tummy)

Cookies, cookies in my tummy!

All gone!
(wave good-bye!)

STORIES TO READ AND SHARE

Hutchins, Pat. *The Doorbell Rang*

Numeroff, Laura Joffe. *If You Give a Mouse a Cookie*

Wagner, Karen. *Chocolate Chip Cookies*

Wellington, Monica. *Mr. Cookie Baker*

Cookies

CRAFT

Cookie-Cutter Shapes

Supplies

Assorted cookie cutters
Crayon or pencil
Scissors
Paper

Collect cookie cutters in different shapes. With a crayon or pencil, have children trace shapes on to paper. Color and decorate. Cut out and display.

Paper Chocolate Chip Cookies

Supplies

Brown construction paper
Circular item to trace
Pencil
Scissors
Black crayon or Magic Marker

Trace circles on brown construction paper. Cut out. Add "chocolate chips" with black crayon or marker.

ACTIVITIES

- Read *Mr. Cookie Baker* (see *Stories to Read and Share*). Make cookies using recipe at back of book.

- For a baking "shortcut," buy slice-and-bake cookies and bake!

- Visit a bakery or have a baker visit your group.

- "Rewrite" the story *If You Give a Mouse a Cookie* by creating the story *If You Give a Kid a Cookie*!

- Using the cookie-cutter shapes (see *Craft*), create a cookie tree and hang creations on branches.

- Adapt the story *If You Give a Mouse a Cookie* to a flannelboard presentation.

- "Roll" cookie dough, "mix," and "stir."

- Use soft clay to create "cookies"; name your creations!

- Bring in baking utensils . . . "show and tell"!

Cowboys

FINGERPLAY/ACTION RHYME

Cowboy Bill

See Cowboy Bill ride his horse,
(pretend to ride a horse)
He wears a hat and boots, of course!
(touch head, touch feet)

Through the prairie he does roam,
(look around)
Far away from his old ranch home.
(point far away)

Giddy-up, giddy-up, be on your way,
(hold horse reins)
Tomorrow is another day!
(nod head "yes")

STORIES TO READ AND SHARE

Etow, Carole, ill. *Cowboy Pup*

Gardella, Tricia. *Just Like My Dad*

Hooker, Ruth. *Matthew the Cowboy*

Rounds, Glen. *Cowboys*

Stadler, John. *The Ballad of Wilbur and the Moose*

Teague, Mark. *How I Spent My Summer Vacation*

Cowboys

 CRAFT

Wild West Collage

Supplies

Old magazines
Paper
Glue
Scissors
Stickers (western)
Star stickers

Look through old magazines for pictures with a western theme. Cut out. Glue on to paper to make collage. Add western stickers and star stickers to complete the western look!

ACTIVITIES

- "Ride" a horse, "perform" lasso tricks.
- Learn a simple country-and-western line dance.
- Visit a ranch or a farm; ride a real horse!
- Invite a real cowboy/cowgirl to visit.
- Have cowboy and cowgirl dress-up days; wear hats, boots, bandanas.
- Decorate program area or classroom in a farm/barn theme.
- Grow cactus from seed.
- Have a barbeque . . . serve hot dogs, beans, toasted marshmallows.
- Play country-and-western music.
- If you know someone who can play a guitar, invite them to perform!

 Cows

FINGERPLAY/ACTION RHYME

Cows

Cows swish their tails all in a line,
(sway back and forth)
Cows in the meadow looking so fine.
(smile)

Cows say, "Moo-moo, where's our lunch?"
(moo)
Cows so hungry go munch-munch!
(chew)

STORIES TO READ AND SHARE

Dubanevich, Arlene. *Calico Cows*

Ericcson, Jennifer A. *No Milk!*

Harrison, David. *When Cows Come Home*

Lindbergh, Reeve. *There's a Cow in the Road*

Loomis, Christine. *One Cow Coughs*

Most, Bernard. *Cock-a-Doodle-Moo!*

Speed, Toby. *Two Cool Cows*

Zidrou. *Ms. Blanche, the Spotless Cow*

Cows

CRAFT

Cowbell

Supplies

Craft cowbells
Ribbon

String a ribbon through top of cowbell, tie. Children can wear around their necks.

OPTIONAL: Paint cowbells in a cow pattern!

ACTIVITIES

 Visit a dairy farm and make arrangements to milk a cow or observe a milking.

- "Milk" a cow, moo-o-o-o!

Conduct a mooing contest!

- Learn about the nutritional value of milk; find out all about milk products.

- Use "Cows" fingerplay to introduce snack time; serve milk and cow-shaped cookies.

- Read *Two Cool Cows* (see *Stories to Read and Share*) and act out with cow puppets. Tie cow-patterned bandana around neck; wear sunglasses like cows in the story.

- Have a "Cool Cow Day." Ask children to dress in their "coolest" attire! Wear black and white, brown and white!

- Decorate program area or classroom like a barn.

- Read *Cock-a-Doodle-Moo!* (see *Stories to Read and Share*) for a humorous treat! Imitate sounds!

☆ Crayons

FINGERPLAY/ACTION RHYME

Crayons, Crayons

Crayons, crayons, standing in line,
(stand tall)
Crayons, crayons, looking so fine.
(smile)

Colors so pretty, colors so bright,
(turn around and pretend to "show off")
Colors to draw a rainbow kite!
(pretend to draw)

STORIES TO READ AND SHARE

Charles, Oz. *How Is a Crayon Made?*

Gilliland, Judith Heide. *Not in the House, Newton!*

Hubbard, Patricia. *My Crayons Talk*

Jeschke, Susan. *Angela and Bear*

Johnson, Crockett. *Harold and the Purple Crayon*

Sachar, Louis. *Monkey Soup*

Crayons

 CRAFT

Crayon Capers

Supplies

Paper
Different types of crayons: Sparkles
                                         Glitter
                                         Glow-in-the-dark
                                         Classic
                                         Rainbow

Give each child a piece of paper and an assortment of crayons. Invite children to use their imaginations and create a work of art all their own!

ACTIVITIES

- Visit a crayon factory to see how crayons are made; if a factory is not nearby, write to one and suggest new colors.
- Put a bunch of crayons in a giant jar and ask children to guess how many are inside. Give the winner the jar as a gift.
- Conduct a "crayon hunt." Hide crayons all over your program area or classroom, see who can find the most!
- Hide a crayon in a box. Give hints throughout your presentation as to what color it is. Reveal at the end of your presentation or at the end of the day.

Dance

FINGERPLAY/ACTION RHYME

Dancing

Dancing is fun, dancing is neat,
Dancing is exercise for my feet.
(tap feet on the ground)

Watch me twirl, watch me twist,
(twirl, "twist")
Dancing is number one on my list!
(show number one by holding up index finger)

STORIES TO READ AND SHARE

Asch, Frank. *Moondance*

Auch, Mary Jane. *Peeping Beauty*

Giannini, Enzo. *Zorina Ballerina*

Hampshire, Susan. *Rosie's Ballet Slippers*

Hoff, Syd. *Duncan the Dancing Duck*

Lowery, Linda. *Twist with a Burger, Jitter with a Bug*

Patrick, Denise Lewis. *Red Dancing Shoes*

Walsh, Ellen Stoll. *Hop Jump*

Dance

CRAFT

Ribbon Dance Ribbons

Supplies

Wooden dowel
Crepe streamers
Tape

Using tape, attach a long crepe paper streamer to a wooden dowel. Put on some music and dance with your new creation!

ACTIVITIES

• Invite a local dancer to visit and perform, and to teach a few dance steps in his/her dance specialty.

• If there's a dance group in your area, attend a performance.

- Collect pictures of dancing shoes (or the real thing) such as ballet slippers, tap shoes, jazz shoes, or cowboy boots (for country line dancing). Display and discuss.

- Learn about different types of dancing such as ballet, jazz, folk, modern, country-and-western.

- Create your own dance and give it a name! Play all different types of music; have children experiment with different moves.

• If any children in your group take dance lessons, invite them to perform.

- Use dance ribbons (see *Craft*) to create an original dance set to music of your choice.

• Put on music from the 1950s and give children hula hoops!

• Dance the following party dances: Twist, YMCA, Macarena, Electric Slide, Hokey Pokey, Bunny Hop, Alley Cat. Don't forget to videotape all of the action!

Eggs

FINGERPLAY/ACTION RHYME

Eggs

Birds lay eggs, turtles do, too,
(flap wings, creep like a turtle)
Eggs can be white, brown, or blue.

Eggs can be scrambled, eggs can be fried,
(scramble eggs, fry eggs)
When spring comes, they are dyed!
(pretend to "dip" egg)

STORIES TO READ AND SHARE

Ernst, Lisa Campbell. *Zinnia and Dot*

Hayes, Sarah. *Bad Egg*

Imai, Miko. *Little Lumpty*

Lorenz, Lee. *Dinah's Egg*

Reiser, Lynn. *The Surprise Family*

Eggs

CRAFT

Eggs-traordinary Eggs

Supplies

White construction paper
Scissors
Crayons
Confetti
Stickers
Glitter
Sequins
Pom-poms
Any miscellaneous decorating items of your choice
Glue

Cut large oval shapes out of white construction paper. Using an assortment of the above-mentioned decorating items, decorate egg.

ACTIVITIES

- Crack open an egg; show yolk, white, membrane.

- Dye eggs.

- Have an egg hunt: Hide plastic eggs all over program area or classroom. Fill with surprises such as candy, small toys, erasers, stickers, etc.

- Serve eggs.

- Make a list of foods that contain eggs.

- Discuss animals that lay eggs such as birds, chickens, turtles, frogs, alligators, and ducks.

- Have an "Egg Roll" relay race: Roll plastic eggs to the finish line! What team will win?

- In the springtime, look for eggshells on the ground.

- "Hatch" out of an egg!

Eyeglasses

FINGERPLAY/ACTION RHYME

Eyeglasses

I wear eyeglasses on the tip of my nose,
(point to nose)
When I look down I can see my toes!
(point to toes while looking down)

Eyeglasses help me to see things both far and near,
(make circles with index fingers and thumbs to form eyeglasses)
Eyeglasses help me to see things oh so clear.
(put "eyeglasses" to eyes)

I like my eyeglasses, I really do,
(nod head)
Eyeglasses are good for me and you!
(point to yourself, point to someone else)

STORIES TO READ AND SHARE

Cousins, Lucy. *What Can Rabbit See?*

Geoghegan, Adrienne. *Dogs Don't Wear Glasses*

Hest, Amy. *Baby Duck and the Bad Eyeglasses*

Keller, Holly. *Cromwell's Glasses*

Smith, Lane. *Glasses (Who Needs 'Em?)*

Tusa, Tricia. *Libby's New Glasses*

Wild, Margaret. *All the Better to See You With!*

Eyeglasses

CRAFT

Paper Monocles

Supplies

Small circular object
Poster board
Pencil
Scissors
Colored cellophane paper
Ribbon or yarn
Tape

Trace a small circular object on to poster board (small enough to fit over a child's eye). Cut out center. Glue colored cellophane paper over middle. With tape, attach a piece of ribbon or yarn. See the world in a different "light"!

ACTIVITIES

- Invite an eye doctor to visit and do a presentation on eye care. Invite parents to attend. Hand out literature.

- Visit an eye doctor's office.

- Collect an assortment of silly toy glasses. Have children try them on! Let them look at themselves in a mirror. Take photos. Display on a bulletin board with the caption "EYE" AM SILLY!

- Discuss the importance of having a positive self-concept for those who wear eyeglasses.

- Demonstrate magnification by having children look through binoculars, magnifying glass.

- Begin an eyeglass collection for those less fortunate.

- Look through a telescope.

- Look through a kaleidoscope.

Feathers

FINGERPLAY/ACTION RHYME

Feathers, Feathers

Feathers here, feathers there,
(point left, point right)
Feathers, feathers everywhere!
(look all around)

Feathers, feathers in my hair,
(fluff hair)
Feathers in the wind without a care.
(blow!)

Feathers here, feathers there,
(point left, point right)
Feathers, feathers everywhere!
(look all around)

STORIES TO READ AND SHARE

Chermayeff, Catherine, and Nan Richardson. *Feathery Facts*
Ehlert, Lois. *Feathers for Lunch*
O'Connor, Karen. *The Feather Book*
Weiss, Leatie. *Heather's Feathers*

Feathers

CRAFT

Feather Painting

Supplies

Large craft feather
Nontoxic paint
White construction paper

Give each child a piece of white construction paper. Using large craft feather as a "brush," paint a picture.

Feather Writing

Supplies

Large craft feather
Nontoxic paint
White construction paper

Dip feather in paint using quill end. Write/print as in days gone by.

ACTIVITIES

- Read *Feathers for Lunch* (see *Stories to Read and Share*). Use the bird guide at the end of the story to help children identify some common backyard feathered friends.

- Look outside for feathers on the ground. Display findings.

- Explain how different types of feathers help a bird to survive. (Some feather types: flight, contour, down, etc.)

- Make your program area or classroom into an aviary. Display as many pictures of birds as you can find.

- Invite an ornithologist to visit and bring some of his/her feathered friends.

- Visit the birdhouse in a zoo.

- Put on soft music and "float" as lightly as a feather!

- Buy a feathered friend for your program area or classroom. Always take good care of your new friend.

- Discuss how Native Americans use feathers for decoration.

- Read *Heather's Feathers* to help explain the concept of bird molting (see *Stories to Read and Share*).

Firefighters

FINGERPLAY/ACTION RHYME

Fireman

A fireman fights fires all over town,
(pretend to use hose)
A fireman helps to keep us safe and sound.
(hug yourself)

He drives a big red truck with a siren so loud,
(drive truck, make a siren noise)
He's my friend and I'm so proud!
(pretend to shake hands)

STORIES TO READ AND SHARE

Chlad, Dorothy. *When There Is a Fire Go Outside*

Etow, Carole, ill. *Fireman Bear*

Gibbons, Gail. *Fire! Fire!*

Kraus, Robert. *Owliver*

Martin, Bill, Jr. *"Fire! Fire!" Said Mrs. McGuire*

Rockwell, Anne. *Fire Engines*

Firefighters

CRAFT

Firehouse

Supplies

White construction paper
Crayons
Magic Markers, firefighter stickers

On white construction paper sketch the outline of a firehouse. Using crayons and markers, fill in details. Add stickers where desired. Send as a "thank you" to your local fire department!

ACTIVITIES

- Invite a firefighter to visit and discuss fire safety. Have parents present.
- Visit your town's firehouse for a tour.
- Make fire safety posters. Display.
- Learn all about the equipment on a fire truck and what it's used for.
- "Drive" fire truck, "sound" siren, "spray" hose, "climb" ladder.

Fireflies

FINGERPLAY/ACTION RHYME

Little Firefly

Little firefly glowing in the night,
(open, close fingers)
Little firefly, oh so bright.
(continue to open, close fingers)

Twinkling here, twinkling there,
(flutter fingers)
Twinkle, twinkle everywhere!
(open arms)

STORIES TO READ AND SHARE

Carle, Eric. *The Very Lonely Firefly*
Eastman, P. D. *Sam and the Firefly*
London, Jonathan. *Fireflies, Fireflies, Light My Way*

Fireflies

CRAFT

Firefly T-Shirt

Supplies

Old T-shirt
Glow-in-the-dark fabric paint

On old T-shirt (make sure that it has been washed), apply glow-in-the-dark paint in little circles all over. Let dry. Expose to light. Turn off the lights . . . watch the "fireflies" glow!

ACTIVITIES

- Read *The Very Lonely Firefly* (see *Stories to Read and Share*) for some instant firefly "magic" (fireflies lit by a battery glow at the end of the story).

- Discuss how fireflies really glow.

- Name things that glow or light up: the sun, moon, stars, lightbulbs, holiday lights, fire, flashlight fish, fireworks, night-lights, etc.

- Give each child a glow stick (this will be their own personal firefly). Name each firefly. Have a "Firefly Fly": Put on soft music, put out the lights, and wave glow sticks as if fireflies were flying! Buy sticks in assorted colors for some "special" effects! (Some firefly species actually glow in different colors.) Wear firefly T-shirts for this event (see *Craft*).

- Observe a firefly up close. Capture gently, inspect, then let go.

Frogs

FINGERPLAY/ACTION RHYME

Croaky Croaker

Croaky Croaker the great green frog,
(stand tall)
Croaky Croaker sitting on a log.
(sit)

Catchin' a fly, catchin' a flea,
("catch" a fly, "catch" a flea)
Croaky Croaker, don't catch me!
(shake head)

STORIES TO READ AND SHARE

Arnold, Tedd. *Green Wilma*

Faulkner, Keith. *The Wide-Mouthed Frog*

Gordon, Margaret. *Frogs' Holiday*

London, Jonathan. *Froggy Learns to Swim*

Parker, Nancy Winslow. *Working Frog*

Frogs

CRAFT

Paper Plate Frog

Supplies

Paper plate
Crayons
Pom-poms
Red construction paper
String
Tape
Glue
"Fake" bug

Color a paper plate green or whatever color you desire frog to be. Fold paper plate in half. Glue pom-poms on top to make eyes. Cut a "tongue" out of red construction paper. Glue in mouth area. Cut a piece of string to desired length. Tie fake bug on one end of string. Tape the other end of string inside frog's mouth. By moving hand, try to make frog "catch" bug!

ACTIVITIES

- "Croak" and "rib-it"! "Catch" insects!

- Have a leaping frog contest: How far can you leap? Measure.

- During the spring, take a trip to a local pond and look for frogs.

- Visit an aquarium that has a frog exhibit.

- Have a "Green Frog Day" where everyone wears green. Serve green Jell-O, decorate room in green!

- Discuss frogs and tadpoles far and near. Include frogs of the rain forest. Learn about frogs that are red, blue, yellow.

- Read *Frogs' Holiday* (see *Stories to Read and Share*). If you were a frog, where would you go on vacation? Draw a picture of your special vacation place.

- Play "Feed the Frog": Use a barrel, trash can, or bucket as the "frog." Feed frog by tossing in beanbags!

- How many things can you name that are green!

- Create a bulletin board using the caption LEAPFROG INTO A GOOD BOOK.

Hot-Air Balloons

FINGERPLAY/ACTION RHYME

Hot-Air Balloon Ride

Hot-air balloon, give us a ride,
Fly us over the countryside.
(point up)

Hear the burner go whoosh-whoosh,
Feel the wind gently push!
(make burner sounds)

Up to meet the clear blue sky,
As we wave, good-bye, good-bye!
(wave)

STORIES TO READ AND SHARE

Appelt, Kathi. *Elephants Aloft*

Calhoun, Mary. *Hot-Air Henry*

Delacre, Lulu. *Nathan's Balloon Adventure*

Wilson, Sarah. *Three in a Balloon*

Hot-Air Balloons

Craft

Hot-Air Balloon Collage

Supplies

Blue construction paper
Cotton balls
Hot-air balloon stickers
Glue

On blue construction paper, place hot-air balloon stickers in several different sections. Glue cotton balls in between balloons to form sunny-day clouds!

OPTIONAL: Draw in birds!

ACTIVITIES

- Read *Three in a Balloon* (see *Stories to Read and Share*) to introduce children to the first balloon passengers. Surprise children by using puppets of these "passengers": a rooster, a sheep, and a duck!

- Invite a balloonist to visit . . . have an inflation.

- Attend a balloon launch.

- "Float" like a balloon.

- Take an imaginary balloon flight. What do you see? Where would you go? Chart your journey on a map. Celebrate your "landing" with juice and crackers!

- Decorate your program area or classroom with pictures of hot-air balloons.

Ice Cream

FINGERPLAY/ACTION RHYME

Ice Cream

Ice cream is good, it's so yummy,
(rub stomach)
I like ice cream when it's in my tummy!
(point to tummy)

Chocolate, vanilla, and strawberry pink,
(show three fingers)
Give me three scoops, that's enough, don't you think?
(pretend to scoop)

STORIES TO READ AND SHARE

Armitage, Ronda, and David Armitage. *Ice Cream for Rosie*

Henley, Claire. *Joe's Pool*

McKean, Thomas. *Hooray for Grandma Jo!*

Rey, Margaret. *Curious George Goes to an Ice Cream Shop*

Ice Cream

CRAFT

Ice-Cream Cone Picture

Supplies

Brown construction paper
Pastel construction paper
Glue
Scissors
Red pom-pom
Confetti
Glitter
Magic Markers
Polyester craft fiberfill or cotton balls

Cut an enlarged triangular shape out of brown construction paper to form cone. Cut out circles from pastel construction paper to make scoops. Glue cone and scoops on to contrasting pastel construction paper. Add red pom-pom to make cherry. Make "sprinkles" with confetti, glitter, or Magic Markers. Use polyester craft fiberfill or cotton balls to make whipped cream.

VARIATIONS: Using the same idea as above, make a sundae, Popsicle, banana split, frosty drink, etc.

ACTIVITIES

- Have an ice-cream social/party. Serve cones, cups, assorted toppings . . . don't forget the sprinkles! Invite families to join the fun!

- Bring in an ice-cream maker and make your own.

- Invent your own sundae; send the idea to an ice-cream company.

- Invent your own flavor and suggest it to an ice-cream company.

- Make the LARGEST cone that you can. On a bulletin board or wall, add a scoop for each child. Write their name on scoop.

- Vote for your favorite flavor. Which one will win?

- Research the history of ice cream.

Koalas

FINGERPLAY/ACTION RHYME

Cuddly Koala

Cuddly koala in the eucalyptus tree,
(point up)
Sitting on Mama's back for all the world to see.
(pat back)

Blue-gum baby hungry for lunch,
(rub tummy)
Lots of green leaves for you to munch.
(pretend to eat)

Eat up little fellow, fill your tummy,
(point to stomach)
Tastes so good, yummy, yummy!
(rub tummy)

STORIES TO READ AND SHARE

Gelman, Rita Golden. *A Koala Grows Up*

Irvine, Georgeanne. *Sydney the Koala*

Pene Dubois, William. *Bear Party*

Snyder, Dick. *One Day at the Zoo*

Koalas

CRAFT

Gum Baby Tree

Supplies

White construction paper
Crayons
Koala stickers

Ask children to draw eucalyptus trees on white construction paper. Place koala stickers on branches. You now have your very own koala park!

ACTIVITIES

- Discuss the fact that koalas are not really bears, but marsupials. Learn about how the babies are carried in pouches. Remember that they are native to Australia and are nocturnal animals.

- Discuss their diet, which consists of eucalyptus leaves. This is how they obtain both food and water. This is why they smell like cough drops!

- Discuss their endangerment.

- Have a "Bear Party." Read the book of the same title (see *Stories to Read and Share*) and come dressed in costume.

- Climb like a koala.

- Learn all about Australia, home of the koala.

- Discuss other animals that have pouches such as the kangaroo and the opossum.

- Invite someone who has visited Australia to meet the children and share stories.

- Play "Guess What's in the Koala's Pouch": Give each child a lunch bag with something special inside. Take a guess and then peek!

- Make a pouch on a bulletin board. Fill it with things for the needy in your area.

 Ladybugs

FINGERPLAY/ACTION RHYME

Ladybug

Ladybug, ladybug, how do you do?
(shake hands)
Ladybug, ladybug, how are you?
(nod head)

Ladybug, ladybug, don't fly away,
(shake head, flap arms)
Ladybug, ladybug, I want to play!
(clap hands)

STORIES TO READ AND SHARE

Bernhard, Emery. *Ladybug*
Carle, Eric. *The Grouchy Ladybug*
Wong, Herbert H., and Matthew F. Vessel. *My Ladybug*

Ladybugs

CRAFT

Ladybug Leaf

Supplies

Green construction paper
Scissors
Crayons
Thin black Magic Marker
Red (round) pressure-sensitive labels

Using green construction paper, draw a leaf shape and cut out. If desired, draw in leaf veins with crayons or marker. Add red pressure-sensitive labels where desired. Using thin black marker, make black ladybug "spots." Draw legs.

Balloon Ladybug

Supplies

Round red balloon
Black Magic Marker

Blow up a red balloon. Tie. Make ladybug "spots" with black Magic Marker. Let it "fly" and "land" by letting the air out. Or fill the balloon with helium and tie a string on it . . . the ladybug will "fly"! Don't let go!

ACTIVITIES

- Ladybugs are believed to bring good luck. Decorate your program area or classroom with paper ladybugs!

- In spring, search for ladybugs; observe their behavior.

- Face paint ladybugs on children's cheeks!

- Discuss how ladybugs help farmers by controlling pesty insects.

- Make posters demonstrating how ladybugs are helpful. Display.

Leopards

FINGERPLAY/ACTION RHYME

Spotted, Dotted Leopard

Spotted, dotted leopard lookin' at me,
(point to yourself)
Spotted, dotted leopard, what do you see?
(shrug shoulders)

A little person who looks just like you?
(point outward)
Can you count my freckles; ready, one, two!
(count)

STORIES TO READ AND SHARE

Maestro, Giulio. *Leopard Is Sick*

Radcliffe, Theresa. *The Snow Leopard*

Richardson, Judith Benet. *Come to My Party*

Leopards

CRAFT

Spotted Leopard Mask

Supplies

Large paper plate
Pencil
Black Magic Marker or crayon
Craft stick
Tape
Optional: Tan crayon
           Tan paint

Using a large paper plate, cut out two circles large enough for eyes. If your plate is white, color or paint it tan or keep it white for a snow leopard. Draw leopard nose, mouth, whiskers using black Magic Marker or crayon. Make leopard spots in the same manner. Attach a craft stick with tape to make a handle. Children can hold mask up to face.

ACTIVITIES

- Discuss different types of leopards, where they live, what they eat, their endangerment, etc. Show pictures.

- Give each child leopard "spots": Use nontoxic black Halloween makeup! Show children what they look like in a mirror!

- Use poster board to make leopard paw prints in your program area or classroom. Have the paw prints lead to a book display about animals. Title your display I'VE SPOTTED A GOOD BOOK!

- Hide several pictures of leopards around your room. Ask children to see how many they can "spot"!

Moles

FINGERPLAY/ACTION RHYME

Mole

A mole is fat and a mole is round,
(make big tummy with hands)
A mole digs a hole deep in the ground.
(dig)

When he is finished, he goes to sleep,
(pretend to sleep)
He makes not a sound, not even a peep!
(put finger to lips)

STORIES TO READ AND SHARE

Edwards, Richard. *Moles Can Dance*

Ehlert, Lois. *Mole's Hill*

Lesser, Carolyn. *Dig Hole, Soft Mole*

Moles

CRAFT

Pom-Pom Mole

Supplies

Extralarge pom-pom
Wiggly eyes
Glue
Brown bag
Small strip of yarn

Glue wiggly eyes to large pom-pom. Add small strip of yarn for tail. "Bury" mole in brown bag!

ACTIVITIES

- "Dig" a mole hole!
- Create a "mole city"!
- Discuss a mole's characteristics.
- Visit a zoo to see a mole up close and personal.
- If you live in an area where moles are common, look for them and observe.
- Read *Moles Can't Dance* (see *Stories to Read and Share*). After reading, do a "mole dance"!

The Moon

FINGERPLAY/ACTION RHYME

The Moon

The moon shines bright for all the world to see.
(make circle with arms)
The moon lights up the night sky for both you and me.
(point to yourself and someone else)

Sometimes it's big,
(stand on toes)
Sometimes it's small,
(squat down)
Sometimes it looks like a shiny beach ball!
(pretend to bounce ball)

STORIES TO READ AND SHARE

Asch, Frank. *Happy Birthday, Moon*

Asch, Frank. *Mooncake*

Asch, Frank. *Moongame*

Brown, Margaret Wise. *Goodnight, Moon Pop-Up Book*

Fowler, Allan. *So That's How the Moon Changes*

Hines, Anna Grossnickle. *Moon's Wish*

Spohn, Kate. *Night Goes By*

Turner, Charles. *The Turtle and the Moon*

Whitcher, Susan. *Moonfall*

The Moon

CRAFT

Moon Glow Shapes

Supplies

White or pale yellow construction paper
Black construction paper
Glue
Glow-in-the-dark paint or crayons

Using white or pale yellow construction paper, cut out moon shapes such as crescent, half moon, quarter moon, full moon. Glue shapes on to black paper. Apply glow-in-the-dark paint or crayons to moon shapes. Turn off the lights and watch the moon glow!

ACTIVITIES

- Discuss moon facts and the phases of the moon.
- Moon "walk" like the astronauts!
- Create an imaginary "moon city." Ask children to imagine what it would be like to live on the moon. Help children to draw and record their thoughts on paper.
- Create moon stories. Publish in a booklet.
- Create a "moon dance." Use soft music as background.
- Give the moon a name!
- Read *Moongame* (see *Stories to Read and Share*). Afterward, play moon hide-and-seek. Hide a white or yellow ball or balloon. Give hints as to the moon's whereabouts. Winner gets ball or balloon as prize.
- Host a birthday party for the moon after reading *Happy Birthday, Moon* (see *Stories to Read and Share*). Decorate with streamers, moon shapes, etc. Wear party hats. (If you so desire, you can make paper top hats for everyone like in the story.) Sing "Happy Birthday."
- Play "Pin the Spaceship on the Moon."
- Read *Mooncake* (see *Stories to Read and Share*), then make a round "mooncake" and frost with white or yellow icing.

✦ Moose

FINGERPLAY/ACTION RHYME

Moose

There's a moose on the loose, this I know,
(look all around)
I see him running through the snow.
(run in place)

He is big and he is fast,
(open arms to show big)
If I race him, I'll come in last!
(make a sad face)

STORIES TO READ AND SHARE

Carlstrom, Nancy. *Moose in the Garden*

Day, David. *King of the Woods*

Numeroff, Laura Joffe. *If You Give a Moose a Muffin*

Stapler, Sarah. *Spruce the Moose Cuts Loose*

West, Colin. *"I Don't Care!" Said the Bear*

Moose

CRAFT

Moose Antlers

Supplies

Brown poster board
Scissors
Stapler

Cut antler shapes out of brown poster board. Cut a strip of poster board to make a band that will fit around a child's head. Staple antlers to band. Staple band together. Place on child's head.

ACTIVITIES

- Make moose calls!

- Read all about moose. Find out where they live, what they eat, etc.

- Read *If You Give a Moose a Muffin* (see *Stories to Read and Share*). Have children wear antlers (see *Craft*). Serve muffins.

- Have a "Moose Day": serve chocolate "moose" (pudding or yogurt)!

Parakeets, Parrots

FINGERPLAY/ACTION RHYME

Percy Parakeet

Percy Parakeet, oh so sweet,
(hug yourself)
Percy Parakeet has no teeth!
(point to teeth)

He can dance and he can talk,
(dance, open and close mouth)
Percy Parakeet sure can squawk!
(screech)

Pretty Parrot

I see a pretty parrot in the tall jungle tree,
(look up)
Oh, pretty parrot, will you look at me?
(point to yourself)

Your rainbow feathers in the sun do shine,
(make sun with arms)
Oh, pretty parrot, you are so fine!
(strut)

STORIES TO READ AND SHARE

Banchek, Linda. *Snake In, Snake Out*

Cressey, James. *Pet Parrot*

Demuth, Patricia Brennan. *Max, the Bad-Talking Parrot*

Gordon, Sharon. *Pete the Parakeet*

Lester, Helen. *Princess Penelope's Parrot*

Mahy, Margaret. *The Horrendous Hullabaloo*

Parakeets, Parrots

CRAFT

Parakeet/Parrot Feet

Supplies

Poster board, any color
Scissors
Yarn
Tape

Cut out the shape of bird's feet from poster board (large enough for child). Attach yarn on either side of each foot with tape. Tie around child's feet. Walk like a parakeet!

ACTIVITIES

- Learn all about parakeets and parrots, their origin, food requirements, etc.
- Visit a pet shop.
- Invite a parakeet/parrot owner to bring his/her feathered friend to your program area or classroom.
- Visit a zoo's birdhouse.
- "Squawk," imitate a parakeet's/parrot's antics!
- Learn good pet care.

Penguins

FINGERPLAY/ACTION RHYME

Seven Chubby Penguins

Seven chubby penguins doing splash kicks,
One went swimming and then there were six.

Six chubby penguins performing high dives,
One went skating and then there were five.

Five chubby penguins knocking on my door,
One went skiing and then there were four.

Four chubby penguins heading for the sea,
One went surfing and then there were three.

Three chubby penguins making fish stew,
One went sledding and then there were two.

Two chubby penguins sitting in the sun,
One went tobogganing and then there was
     one.

One chubby penguin sitting all alone,
One chubby penguin wobbled on home!

(act out fingerplay by counting on fingers;
act out other motions if so desired)

STORIES TO READ AND SHARE

Benson, Patrick. *Little Penguin*

Cowcher, Helen. *Antarctica*

Gravois, Jeanne. *Quickly, Quigley*

McMillan, Bruce. *Puffins Climb, Penguins Rhyme*

Weiss, Leatie. *Funny Feet!*

Winteringham, Victoria. *Penguin Day*

Penguins

CRAFT

Penguin Snow Scene

Supplies

Blue construction paper
White crayon and/or chalk
Penguin stickers

On blue construction paper, draw snow, icebergs, and other winter scenery. Place penguin stickers where desired. If other arctic animal stickers are available, add to the scene.

OPTIONAL: Use a glow-in-the-dark crayon to create a "night scene."

ACTIVITIES

- Walk, swim, dive, wobble, hop, and flap wings like a penguin to some upbeat music!

- Dress in black and white! Host a "Penguin Day" complete with a "penguin parade"!

- Learn all about the different species of penguins.

- Invent a penguin line dance!

- Adapt fingerplay (see *Fingerplay/Action Rhyme*) to flannelboard.

- Have a penguin race . . . "wobble" to the finish line!

- Host a "penguin picnic": Serve ice cream, yogurt, gummy fish, Popsicles, etc.

- Read *Penguin Day* (see *Stories to Read and Share*). Have children compare story with their daily activities.

Pockets

FINGERPLAY/ACTION RHYME

Sammy Crocket

Sammy Crocket has a pocket, as big as big can be,
(show big with hands)
Sammy Crocket's big, big pocket reaches to his knee!
(point to knee)

What's in your pocket, Sammy, what do you hide?
(shrug shoulders)
Open your pocket, show what's inside!
(peek in pocket)

STORIES TO READ AND SHARE

Carter, David A. *What's in My Pocket?*

Freeman, Don. *A Pocket for Corduroy*

Ravilious, Robin. *Two in a Pocket*

Pockets

CRAFT

Construction Paper Pocket

Supplies

Construction paper, any color
Stapler
Stickers
Crayons

Staple together two pieces of construction paper on three sides. Children can color and decorate with stickers and crayons. Ask each child to hide something special in their pocket.

ACTIVITIES

- Learn about animals with "pockets," marsupials such as koalas, kangaroos, opossums, etc.

- Play "What's in My Pocket?": Wear clothing with pockets and hide small objects in them. Have children guess what's inside. (Suggested objects: pencils, small stuffed animals, books, crayons, special snacks, stickers, and rulers.)

- Pretend to hide in a pocket . . . "pop" out!

- Create imaginary animals/creatures with pockets; give them names. What's inside their pockets!

- Create a bulletin board filled with pockets (one for each child). Fill with special surprises on special days. Ask each child to design their own bulletin board pocket.

Police Officers

FINGERPLAY/ACTION RHYME

Mr. Policeman

Mr. Policeman dressed in blue,
("brush" off uniform)
I'm very pleased to meet you!
(smile)

You are my friend, let's shake hands,
(shake hands)
Because you are the finest in the land!
(open arms out wide)

STORIES TO READ AND SHARE

Adelson, Leone. *Who Blew That Whistle?*

Keats, Ezra Jack. *My Dog Is Lost!*

McCloskey, Robert. *Make Way for Ducklings*

Mayer, Mercer. *Policeman Critter*

Rey, Margaret. *Curious George Visits a Police Station*

Police Officers

CRAFT

Police Officer's Badge

Supplies

Poster board
Pencil
Scissors
Crayons
Self-adhesive stars
Tape

Trace the outline of a badge shape on poster board. Cut out. Color and decorate with self-adhesive stars. Write or print child's name on it. Attach to child's shirt with tape.

Whistles

Buy whistles. Attach ribbon. Wear around neck. Blow!

ACTIVITIES

- Invite a police officer to visit. Discuss stranger safety, street safety, bike safety, personal safety. Invite parents to attend with their children.
- "Drive" car, "blow" siren, "direct" traffic.
- Invite an officer from a special policing unit to visit. Consider a police officer on horseback, on bicycle, on a motorcycle, etc.
- Sponsor a safety poster contest; have the entries judged by police officers in your town.
- Write a safety story.
- Visit your town's police department.
- "Fingerprint" with finger paint!
- Purchase whistle lollipops and reward children for safety efforts.

Puppies

FINGERPLAY/ACTION RHYME

My Puppy Sam

Sam is my puppy, he's small and fluffy,
(show small)
He has a long tail, oh so puffy!
(wag tail by wiggling bottom)

Sam can roll over and sit up, too,
(roll over, sit up)
Just watch as he does a special trick for you!
(do a trick!)

Woof-woof!

STORIES TO READ AND SHARE

Anholt, Laurence. *The New Puppy*
Bridwell, Norman. *Clifford's Puppy Days*
Brown, Marc. *Arthur's New Puppy*
Griffith, Helen V. *"Mine Will," Said John*
Grindley, Sally. *Four Black Puppies*
Kopper, Lisa. *Daisy Thinks She Is a Baby*
Mongas, Brian. *Follow That Puppy!*
Szekeres, Cindy. *Puppy Too Small*

Puppies

CRAFT

Puppy Ears

Supplies

Construction paper
Scissors
Stapler
Pencil
Tape

Measure and cut a strip of construction paper to fit comfortably around a child's head. Staple. Cut two ovals to make ears. Staple or tape ears on either side of band. Instant puppy ears!

Dog Collars

Supplies

Construction paper
Scissors
Hole puncher
Yarn
Stickers, stars, etc.
Optional: Glow-in-the-dark paint

Measure and cut a strip of construction paper to fit loosely around child's neck. This will form collar. On another piece of construction paper, cut out the shape of a bone. Using a hole puncher, punch a hole in collar and a hole in the top of bone. Attach bone to collar with a small piece of yarn. Decorate collar with stickers, stars, etc. For a reflector collar, add glow-in-the-dark paint.

ACTIVITIES

- Discuss puppy dog care or visit a vet.

- "Spot-and-dot" your program area or classroom . . . use 101 spots for a dalmatian effect!

- "Roll over," "sit up," "bark," "give paw," "wag tail," create new puppy trick!

- Visit an animal shelter, or set up a collection drive for an animal shelter; collect food, towels, etc. Call your program "Puppy Pals."

- Learn about the different breeds of dogs, as well as different types such as Seeing Eye dogs, sled dogs, etc.

- Using Halloween makeup, put on dalmatian spots, whiskers!

- Put construction paw prints all over your program area or classroom.

- Do a puppy book display; title your display WE PAWS FOR BOOKS.

- Write a puppy tale; publish in a booklet and title it "Paws to Read."

- Host a "Draw Your Favorite Dog" contest.

- Play "Pin the Ears and Tail on the Puppy."

Raccoons

FINGERPLAY/ACTION RHYME

Five Raccoons

Five raccoons fat and round,
(show "fat" with arms making a tummy)
Five raccoons not making a sound.
(put fingers to lips)

Dressed in stripes from tip to tail,
(shake "tail")
Slinking in the moonlight, oh, so pale.
(slink)

Five raccoons walking in a line,
(walk)
Five raccoons looking so fine!
(smile)

STORIES TO READ AND SHARE

Arnosky, Jim. *Raccoons and Ripe Corn*

Burdick, Margaret. *Sara Raccoon and the Secret Place*

McPhail, David. *Something Special*

Wells, Rosemary. *Timothy Goes to School*

Raccoons

CRAFT

Raccoon Mask

Supplies

Black poster board or construction paper
Scissors
String or yarn

Using black poster board or construction paper, cut a strip long enough to fit over upper part of child's face. Cut out holes large enough for eyes (make sure vision is clear). Attach yarn or string on both ends. Tie around child's head.

ACTIVITIES

- Discuss other animals that have stripes besides raccoons. How do stripes help to protect them?
- Discuss characteristics of the raccoon. Learn about its food requirements, how it cares for its young, etc.
- Play "Pin the Tail on the Raccoon" as you would play "Pin the Tail on the Donkey."
- Create a dance called the "Rockin' Raccoon!"
- Adapt fingerplay to a flannelboard (see *Fingerplay/Action Rhyme*).
- Walk in a line!
- Adapt fingerplay (see *Fingerplay/Action Rhyme*) to a glove puppet using pom-poms and wiggly eyes to make raccoons.

The Sea

FINGERPLAY/ACTION RHYME

The Seashore

The waves splash as they reach the shore,
(sway back and forth)
I catch one and wait for more!
("catch" with hands)

I look for shiny seashells,
(look)
And listen to the sound of the buoy bells.
(cup hand to ear)

I build castles made of sand,
(pretend to build)
Mom and Dad lend a hand.
(hold out hand)

Seagulls squawk as they fly by,
(squawk)
Look at them so high in the sky.
(look up)

Dolphins leap far, far away,
(leap and dive)
Sun goes down on a fun, fun day!
(make circle with arms, make sun "set")

STORIES TO READ AND SHARE

Asch, Frank. *Sand Cake*

Craig, Janet. *What's Under the Ocean*

O'Donnell, Elizabeth Lee. *The Twelve Days of Summer*

Rockwell, Anne. *At the Beach*

Seymour, Peter. *What's at the Beach?*

Seymour, Peter. *What's in the Deep Blue Sea?*

Stock, Catherine. *Sophie's Bucket*

The Sea

CRAFT

Starfish Stick Puppet

Supplies

Sandpaper
Scissors
Pencil
Craft stick
Tape

Trace a starfish shape on to sandpaper. Cut out. Tape a craft stick on the back. Make your starfish crawl!

Sponge Print Art

Supplies

Sponges
Scissors
Construction paper
Paint

Cut sea shapes out of sponges. Dip in paint and "print" on construction paper.

ACTIVITIES

- Host a "Seashore Day": wear swimwear; bring a beach umbrella, towels, sunglasses; read stories. On a plastic tablecloth, pour sand and dampen. Make sand sculptures using assorted buckets, cookie cutters, etc.
- Decorate program area or classroom like a beach. Hang paper gulls from the ceiling.
- Bring in a small inflatable pool. Fill with water and host a "Splish Splash"! (If doing this indoors, cover things with large plastic tablecloths or covers.)
- Serve gummy fish, fish-shaped pretzels and crackers, seashell pasta.
- Set up an aquarium; observe sea life.
- Learn about the creatures that live in the sea. Discuss different types of seashells. Give each child a seashell to keep . . . listen for the swoosh of the ocean! Conduct a seashell counting contest.
- Blow fish bubbles! Using giant bubble pan, blow whale bubbles!
- Invite a lifeguard or coast guard member to speak about sea safety.
- "Swim," "dive," "row" a boat, "surf," "water-ski," squawk like a gull, imitate the sounds of the sea.
- Play the sounds of the sea on CD or cassette. Play a video of an aquarium or ocean scene.

 Shoes

FINGERPLAY/ACTION RHYME

Shoes

Pink shoes, red shoes, purple shoes, too,
(point to your shoes)
Fat ones, skinny ones, all for you.
(point to yourself)

Big shoes, baby shoes, and those in between,
(make big with hands, make small with hands)
I like my shoes pea pickle green!
(point to yourself)

STORIES TO READ AND SHARE

Fox, Mem. *Shoes from Grandpa*

Hampshire, Susan. *Rosie's Ballet Slippers*

Riddell, Chris. *Bird's New Shoes*

Tafuri, Nancy. *Two New Sneakers*

Weiss, Leatie. *Funny Feet!*

Shoes

CRAFT

Shoe Prints

Supplies

Pencil
Construction paper or poster board
Crayons and assorted decorating items
Scissors

Trace outline of child's shoes. Cut out. Color and decorate.

ACTIVITIES

- Collect different types of shoes and/or pictures of them. Some suggestions: work boots, sneakers, sandals, ice skates, ballet slippers, cowboy boots, high heels, fishing boots, snowshoes, firefighter boots, track shoes. Invite people who wear the above to discuss what they do.

- Ask each child to bring in or wear his/her favorite shoes on "Favorite Shoes Day"!

- Bring in a few old shoes. Decorate and design unique creations! Use sequins, paint, Magic Markers, pom-poms, stickers, crayons, etc. Display.

- Give instruction on how to lace and tie shoes.

- Design a bulletin board using the caption PUT YOUR BEST FOOT FORWARD.

- Display shoe prints (see *Craft*) and invite parents to come in and guess which print belongs to their child.

Snakes

FINGERPLAY/ACTION RHYME

Green Snake

S-s-s-slithering, s-s-s-slinking, silly green snake,
(wiggle)
In the sun a bath did take.
("wash" yourself)

He s-s-s-splished and he s-s-s-splashed until he was clean,
(splish and splash)
Silly green snake, s-s-s-so long and s-s-s-so lean!
(stretch arms out to show length)

STORIES TO READ AND SHARE

Ata, Te. *Baby Rattlesnake*

Gray, Libba Moore. *Small Green Snake*

Kudrna, C. Imbior. *To Bathe a Boa*

Tate, Lindsey. *Claire and the Friendly Snakes*

Walsh, Ellen Stoll. *Mouse Count*

Warren, Cathy. *Victoria's ABC Adventure*

Snakes

CRAFT

Slinky the Snake

Supplies

Nontoxic clay
Miscellaneous decorative objects such as large craft beads, sequins, buttons

Using nontoxic clay, roll and stretch out. When desired length is reached, curve, curl, or coil it into a snake. Make "skin" using any of the above decorative items.

Rattlesnake Rattle

Supplies

Paper or plastic bathroom cups
Dried beans
Tape

Fill a paper or plastic cup with a small amount of dried beans. Take another cup of the same size and place it over the opening of the bean-filled cup. Tape the two cups together securely. Shake for a "rattling" sound!

ACTIVITIES

- Invite a herpetologist to visit with the children and ask him/her to bring some wiggly friends!

- Wiggle and slither on the ground like a snake. Hiss!

- Read *Baby Rattlesnake* (see *Stories to Read and Share*) and accompany your presentation with the baby rattlesnakes's rattle using a baby rattle. Let each child take a turn shaking the rattle.

- Turn your group of children into a large snake by lining them up and slithering around the room. Give your super-sized snake a name!

- Encourage children to "coil" up with a good story!

- Decorate your program area or classroom with a giant balloon snake. Blow up your favorite color balloons. Using double-sided tape, tape balloons together to form a long wiggly snake. Disassemble at the end of your presentation and give each child a balloon to take home. Instant cleanup!

 Snowflakes

FINGERPLAY/ACTION RHYME

Snowflakes

Snowflakes, snowflakes dancing in the air,
(twirl)
Snowflakes, snowflakes kissing my hair.
(throw a kiss)

Snowflakes, snowflakes so cold and white,
(shiver)
Snowflakes, snowflakes falling all night.
(pretend to sleep)

STORIES TO READ AND SHARE

Brown, Margaret Wise. *Animals in the Snow*

Chapman, Cheryl. *Snow on Snow on Snow*

Ehlert, Lois. *Snowballs*

London, Jonathan. *Froggy Gets Dressed*

McKee, David. *Elmer in the Snow*

Stoeke, Janet. *A Hat for Minerva Louise*

Snowflakes

CRAFT

Paper Snowflakes

Supplies

White construction paper
Scissors
Circular object to trace
Pencil
Glue
Optional: Glitter

Trace a circular object the size that you want your snowflake to be. Cut out circle, then fold in half. Cut out little pieces of paper at random on your circle (in other words, make holes!). Open for instant snowflakes!

OPTIONAL: Apply glitter to your snowflake with glue for a frosty effect!

ACTIVITIES

- Decorate program area or classroom with paper snowflakes (see *Craft*). Create a blizzard!

- Host a "Snowflake Day" . . . everyone wear white!

- Guess how many inches/feet of snow will fall during the winter.

- Put on soft music and spin and twirl like snowflakes. Or give each child a white ribbon or paper streamer to whirl around the room.

- Make snowballs or snow people out of white clay.

- Host a "Snow Ball"/winter party. Serve ice cream!

- Build a snow person on your bulletin board or wall: Give each child a white paper circle to color and decorate. Put all of the circles together to make a snow person.

- If there is snow in your area, try to observe a snowflake to see its shape.

- Have a winter readathon: Have each child print the title of his/her favorite book on a paper snowflake and display in a prominent area. Title this creation A BLIZZARD OF BOOKS and encourage the children to read each other's favorites.

- Make "snow": Throw confetti all around!

☆ Stars

FINGERPLAY/ACTION RHYME

Stars in the Sky

The stars in the sky twinkle and blink,
The stars in the sky give me a wink!
(point to sky, wink)

It's time for bed, they seem to say,
Good-night my friends in the Milky Way!
(put hands together and rest head)

STORIES TO READ AND SHARE

Asch, Frank. *Starbaby*

Gibbons, Gail. *Stargazers*

Hines, Anna Grossnickle. *Sky All Around*

Karlin, Nurit. *The Tooth Witch*

Spohn, Kate. *Night Goes By*

Stone, Kazuko G. *Aligay Saves the Stars*

Stone, Kazuko G. *Good Night Twinklegator*

Stars

CRAFT

 Twinkle Star Stick Puppet

Supplies

Construction paper or poster board
Star shape to trace
Pencil
Glow-in-the-dark paint
Craft stick
Tape

Cut star shape out of construction paper or poster board. Using glow-in-the-dark paint, apply to stars. Let dry. When dry, attach a craft stick to back of star with tape.

ACTIVITIES

 • Sing "Twinkle, Twinkle, Little Star."

• Decorate program area or classroom with glow-in-the-dark stars that are either purchased or made (see *Craft*). Turn off the lights and watch the "show"!

• Create a constellation in your classroom by having each child design his/her own personal star. Display all together on wall or bulletin board and caption the display WE ALL SHINE IN OUR OWN SPECIAL WAY.

• Discuss what makes a star twinkle.

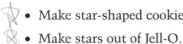 • Make star-shaped cookies for a snack.

• Make stars out of Jell-O.

• Ask children to look all around them to find star shapes.

• Encourage each child to "wish upon a star"!

• Give each child a piece of construction paper, self-adhesive stars, glitter, and glue. If you so desire, also use glitter crayons. Ask them to create their very own sparkling galaxy!

Sunflowers

FINGERPLAY/ACTION RHYME

Sunny Sunflowers

Sunny sunflowers all in a row,
Sunny sunflowers nodding hello!
(nod head)

Growing in my garden, oh so high,
Reaching up, up to the blue, blue sky.
(point up)

In the fall, you will surely turn to seed,
(make tiny seed by holding out pinky)
And lots of hungry birds you will feed!
(flap arms to make wings)

STORIES TO READ AND SHARE

Ford, Miela. *Sunflower*

Howard, Ellen. *The Big Seed*

Stewart, Dianne. *Gift of the Sun: A Tale from South Africa*

Sunflowers

CRAFT

Yardstick Sunflower

Supplies

Yardstick
Green paint
Brown, yellow, and green construction paper
  or poster board
Scissors
Pencil
Tape or glue
Paintbrush
Optional: Fuzzy craft bee

Paint yardstick green (this will be the sun-flower's stem). Cut a circular object out of brown construction paper or poster board. Cut petals out of yellow construction paper or poster board. Attach petals all around brown circle with tape or glue to make the sunflower. Attach the sunflower to yardstick with tape. Cut large leaves out of green construction paper or poster board. Attach to yardstick at intervals with tape.

OPTIONAL: Add a fuzzy craft bee to your flower! (My sunflowers always seem to have a bee in the center!)

ACTIVITIES

- Get a head start on spring: Plant sunflower seeds in containers inside and then transfer them outside when the weather warms up. (See instructions on seed packet.)

- Measure your sunflower's daily growth. Take weekly photos. Display.

- Give each child a seed packet to take home and plant. Encourage children to record progress.

- Taste sunflower seeds.

- Put sunflower seeds outside for birds and small animals to enjoy.

- Discuss how the sunflower got its name . . . by following the sun!

- Observe the creatures that eat from the sunflower: birds, squirrels, bees, butterflies, insects.

- Discuss the different types of sunflowers.

- Use yardstick sunflowers (see *Craft*) to create a sunflower patch in your program area or class-room.

- Discuss how the sunflower is valuable to us for a variety of different products such as food and oil.

# Tigers

FINGERPLAY/ACTION RHYME

Tiger, Tiger

Tiger, tiger, striped orange and black,
Tiger, tiger, swish the tail on your back.
(wiggle backside)

Through the jungle you do walk,
("creep" through the jungle)
What would you say if you could talk?
(shrug shoulders)

STORIES TO READ AND SHARE

Baker, Keith. *Who Is the Beast?*

Cowcher, Helen. *Tigress*

Mogensen, Jan. *The Tiger's Breakfast*

Root, Phyllis. *Moon Tiger*

Wright, Kit. *Tigerella*

Tigers

CRAFT

Paper Plate Tiger Mask

Supplies

Large white paper plate
Orange and black Magic Markers or crayons
Scissors
White construction paper
Stapler
Strips of yarn
Glue
Craft stick
Tape

Using orange and black markers or crayons, make stripes on large white paper plate. Cut out circles for eyes and nose. Draw mouth and make whiskers by gluing on strips of yarn. Make ears out of white construction paper also colored with orange and black stripes. Attach to plate with stapler. Attach craft stick with tape. Hold in front of face. Roar like a tiger!

ACTIVITIES

- "Tiger walk" through the jungle. What do you see?

- Discuss the importance of wildlife conservation and preservation of endangered species. Design posters.

- Make tiger paw prints out of construction paper or poster board. Arrange in program area or classroom. Have the tiger tracks lead to an exhibit of tiger stories (see *Stories to Read and Share*).

- Design a bulletin board using the caption PAWS FOR BOOKS. Create a jungle setting and write each child's name on a paw print along with the name of their favorite book.

- Decorate program area or classroom with black and orange tiger "stripes" (use black and orange streamers).

- Write a "tiger tale"!

- Stripe kids' faces with orange and black Halloween makeup. Don't forget the whiskers!

- Play "Pin the Tail on the Tiger" as you would play "Pin the Tail on the Donkey."

- Discuss how a tiger's stripes help protect it from enemies.

Turkeys

FINGERPLAY/ACTION RHYME

Gobble and Wobble

Gobble and Wobble, two turkeys fair,
Gobble and Wobble have no hair!
(touch top of head)

Instead they wear feathers, head to toe,
Gobble and Wobble are really quite a show!
(point to head, toes)

Gobble likes to sing with the Barnyard Band,
Wobble likes to boogie on the band's
    grandstand!
(sing, dance)

Gobble plays the fiddle, it goes dee-dee,
While the farmer starts a dancin' and slaps his
    knee!
(play fiddle, slap knee)

Wobble strums the banjo, zippy zee,
The farmer is a prancin', see, see, see!
(strum banjo)

Gobble and Wobble two turkeys fair,
Gobble and Wobble such a silly pair!
(wobble back and forth)

STORIES TO READ AND SHARE

Kroll, Steven. *One Tough Turkey: A Thanksgiving Story*
Schatell, Brian. *Farmer Goff and His Turkey Sam*
Schatell, Brian. *Sam's No Dummy, Farmer Goff*
Wickstrom, Sylvie K. *Turkey on the Loose!*

Turkeys

CRAFT

Turkey Stick Puppets

Supplies

Pencil
Poster board
Scissors
Craft feathers
Crayons
Craft stick
Tape
Optional: Wiggly eyes

Trace child's open hand on posterboard. Cut out. Decorate with craft feathers and color. Use wiggly eyes to make turkey's eyes or draw on with crayons. Attach craft stick with tape.

ACTIVITIES

- Gobble and wobble!

- Dance a "turkey trot"!

- Ask children to make turkey faces. Take photos and display on a bulletin board with the caption WE'RE TURKEYS, ARE YOU?

- Visit a turkey farmer to meet these feathered friends up close and personal!

- Play "Pin the Feathers on the Turkey" as you would play "Pin the Tail on the Donkey."

- Have a gobbling contest. Award prizes for the loudest, silliest, most original, most turkeylike!

Turtles

FINGERPLAY/ACTION RHYME

Little Tommy Turtle

Little Tommy turtle sleeping in the sun,
(sleep)
Wake up, Tommy, wake up, it's time for some fun!
(wake up)

If I close my eyes and don't dare peek,
(close eyes)
Will you play hide-and-seek?
(cover eyes with hands, open hands)

STORIES TO READ AND SHARE

Asch, Frank. *Turtle Tale*

Florian, Douglas. *Turtle Day*

Jeffrey, Graham. *Thomas the Tortoise*

McGuire-Turcatte, Casey A. *How Honu the Turtle Got His Shell*

Maris, Ron. *I Wish I Could Fly*

Turner, Charles. *The Turtle and the Moon*

Turtles

CRAFT

Paper Plate Turtle

Supplies

White paper plates
Green paint or crayons
Green construction paper
Large green pom-pom
Glue
Tape
Stapler
Wiggly eyes

Paint or color two white paper plates green. Cut four legs and a tail out of green construction paper. Glue to the inner side of the paper plate. Staple the other on top to make turtle shell. Glue large green pom-pom in place to form head. Add wiggly eyes.

ACTIVITIES

- "Turtle walk," hide inside shell, catch an insect.

- Discuss different types of turtles.

- Name other animals that carry their homes on their backs. Look for pictures.

- Visit an aquarium to see turtles personally.

- Conduct a turtle race by creeping on hands and knees.

- Make a turtle out of clay.

- Play hide-and-seek!

☆ Vegetables

FINGERPLAY/ACTION RHYME

Vegetables

I like carrots, I like peas,
(nod head)
Pass the corn, if you please!
(reach for dish)

I like celery, I like tomatoes,
(nod head)
Mish-mash, pass the potatoes!
(reach for dish)

I like broccoli, and peppers, too,
(nod head)
Vegetables, vegetables, so good for you!

Eat up!
(rub tummy)

STORIES TO READ AND SHARE

Arnosky, Jim. *Raccoons and Ripe Corn*

Caseley, Judith. *Grandpa's Garden Lunch*

Demarest, Chris L. *No Peas for Nellie*

Ehlert, Lois. *Growing Vegetable Soup*

Pelham, David. *Sam's Sandwich*

Rockwell, Anne. *Apples and Pumpkins*

Sobol, Harriet Langsam. *A Book of Vegetables*

Vegetables

CRAFT

Vegetable Garden

Supplies

Brown poster board
Vegetable pictures and/or empty vegetable seed packets
Glue

Using brown poster board as your "garden," cut out pictures of vegetables (or use empty seed packets). Glue in rows to poster board.

Vegetable Faces

Supplies

Construction paper, assorted colors
Crayons or Magic Markers

Cut out assorted vegetable shapes—such as pumpkins, tomatoes, potatoes, corn, cucumbers, carrots—from construction paper. With Magic Markers or crayons, draw faces on the vegetables.

ACTIVITIES

- Read *Growing Vegetable Soup* (see *Stories to Read and Share*) and begin growing vegetables indoors. Have children take home vegetable plants and plant outside in their gardens. Ask children to bring in vegetables to show what they have grown. Or give each child a packet of vegetable seeds to take home.

- Serve vegetable soup as a snack. Ask each child to bring in a vegetable soup ingredient and make your own from scratch! (See recipe in *Growing Vegetable Soup*.) Learn the nutritional value of the assorted vegetables in your soup.

- Sample vegetables that are easy to eat such as raw carrots, celery, peppers, and broccoli. If you have access to a food processor, make juices from vegetables.

- Use your imagination to "grow" a fantasy vegetable garden. Invent names for your creations. Display on bulletin board.

- In the fall, display a pumpkin and ask each child to guess its weight. Award the pumpkin as a prize to the winner. Carve and/or decorate a pumpkin. Give your pumpkin a carrot nose.

- Ask each child to bring a canned vegetable. Make a food basket and donate it to a local food bank.

- Invite a nutritionist to visit.

- Visit a vegetable farm. Explore a cornfield or a pumpkin patch.

- Pretend to plant a garden: rake, hoe, water, pull weeds, pick vegetables, stir vegetable soup, eat!

Whales

FINGERPLAY/ACTION RHYME

Whale

A whale is big and very long,
(show length by stretching arms)
Sometimes a whale can sing a song.
(pretend to sing)

She breathes through a blowhole on the top of her head,
(touch top of head)
And sometimes she dives to the ocean bed.
(dive)

Whales can be blue, white, or gray,
Oh, how I wish I see a whale today!
(pretend to look)

STORIES TO READ AND SHARE

Gibbons, Gail. *Whales*

Hayles, Karen, and Charles Fuge. *Whale Is Stuck*

McMillan, Bruce. *Going on a Whale Watch*

Raffi. *Baby Beluga*

Tokuda, Wendy, and Richard Hall. *Humphrey the Lost Whale*

Weller, Frances Ward. *I Wonder If I'll See a Whale*

Ziefert, Harriet. *Henry's Wrong Turn*

Whales

CRAFT

Paper Bag Whale

Supplies

Lunch bag
Crumpled newspaper
String
Optional: Crayons or paint

Stuff a lunch bag half full with crumpled newspaper. Tie bag above newspaper with string. This forms body and tail. If desired, paint or color bag before beginning. Draw blowhole, eyes, and mouth. Give your whale a name.

ACTIVITIES

- Fill a plant mister with water; squirt to simulate a spouting whale.
 - Display pictures of various whales. Learn their names such as humpback, orca, beluga, etc. Hide pictures in program area or classroom . . . go on a "whale watch" to find them!
- Discuss the importance of marine life conservation and how we can all help.
- Adopt a whale.
- Invite children to write their very own "whale tale"!
- Compose a whale song!
- Pretend to dive, spout, breach, etc.
- Blow whale-sized bubbles!
- Discuss whale migration.
- Invite a marine biologist to visit.

Witches

FINGERPLAY/ACTION RHYME

Three Ugly Witches

Three ugly witches stirring up some brew,
(show three fingers, stir)
Three ugly witches staring at you!
(point to someone)

Long green noses and pointed black hats,
(point to nose, make arms form a pointed hat)
Riding on brooms with big black cats.
(pretend to ride a broom)

Fly away, witches, through the night sky,
(point to sky)
Fly away witches, fly so high.
(fly)

Fly away, witches; far, far away.
(wave good-bye)
Don't forget to come back on Halloween Day!

STORIES TO READ AND SHARE

Bender, Robert. *A Little Witch Magic*

Hutchins, Pat. *Which Witch Is Which?*

Johnston, Tony. *The Witch's Hat*

Karlin, Nurit. *The Tooth Witch*

Meddaugh, Susan. *The Witches' Supermarket*

Nolan, Dennis. *Witch Bazooza*

Witches

CRAFT

Paper Plate Witch Face

Supplies

White paper plate
Crayons
Red or orange yarn
Tape
Scissors
Black construction paper or poster board
Glue
Stapler
Magic Markers

Color a white paper plate green or purple (or other color of your choice). This will be the witch's face. Use red or orange yarn to make witch's hair. Tape on either side of paper plate. Make a witch's hat by cutting a triangle out of black construction paper or poster board. Cut a strip of black paper longer than the widest part of hat to make brim. Glue, tape, or staple along widest part of triangle. Attach completed hat to top of paper plate with stapler. Draw facial features with crayon or Magic Marker. Don't forget the warts!

ACTIVITIES

- Serve "witches brew": juice, soup, punch, etc.

- Dress up like witches: Make available old black hats, old clothes, etc. Add a touch of Halloween makeup!

- "Ride" brooms: Use brooms to clean up your area and have everyone join in!

- Have a broom race!

- Host an ugly witch contest . . . see who can make the ugliest witch (see *Craft*)!

- Write a witch story.

- Read *The Tooth Witch* for a fun explanation of how the stars got in the sky (see *Stories to Read and Share*).

Worms

FINGERPLAY/ACTION RHYME

Wiggly Worm

Wiggly worm, wiggles wiggles,
(wiggle)

Wiggly worm, jiggles jiggles.
(jiggle)

Wiggly worm gives me the giggles giggles!
(laugh)

Stories to Read and Share

Ahlberg, Janet, and Allan Ahlberg. *The Little Worm Book*

Lindgren, Barbro. *A Worm's Tale*

Lionni, Leo. *Inch by Inch*

Pringle, Laurence. *Twist, Wiggle, and Squirm*

Rivlin, Elizabeth. *Elmo's Little Glowworm*

Wong, Herbert H., and Matthew F. Vessel. *Our Earthworms*

Worms

CRAFT

Wiggly Jiggly Worm

Supplies

Slinky
Wiggly eyes
Glue

Attach wiggly eyes to a brightly colored slinky with glue. Instant worm!

Pipe Cleaner Worm

Supplies

Thick pipe cleaner

Bend a thick pipe cleaner into a wiggly shape. Another instant worm!

Glowworm Stick Puppet

Supplies

Poster board
Glow-in-the-dark paint
Wiggly eyes
Craft stick
Tape
Scissors
Glue

Cut a curvy strip of poster board. Apply glow-in-the-dark paint. Let dry. Attach wiggly eyes with glue. Attach craft stick with tape.

ACTIVITIES

- Wiggle and jiggle like a worm . . . do this to some upbeat music to get the wiggles out! Crawl on the floor!

- Learn about earthworms and how they benefit the soil in a garden. Learn how they regenerate.

- In the spring, go outside after a rainstorm and search for worms. Observe their behavior. Capture a few and let them go.

- Serve gummy worms!

- Serve "worms in a can": Heat up some canned pasta!

- Host a wiggling contest!

- Measure things like an inchworm would. Measure your finger, height, arm, leg, nose, etc.

- Host a "Glowworm Glow": Make glowworm stick puppets (see *Craft*) and then turn off the lights, put on some music, and have glowworms dance in the dark!

- Invent a worm squirm!

- Hide a glowworm stick puppet, turn off the lights, and search for him!

Additional Sources

Brown, Marc. *Finger Rhymes.* Ill. by author. New York: Dutton, 1980.

———. *Hand Rhymes.* Ill. by author. New York: Dutton, 1985.

———. *Party Rhymes.* Ill. by author. New York: Dutton, 1988.

———. *Play Rhymes.* Ill. by author. New York: Dutton, 1987.

Cole, Joanna, and Stephanie Calmenson. *The Eentsy, Weentsy Spider: Fingerplays and Action Rhymes.* Ill. by Alan Tiegreen. New York: Morrow, 1991.

Cooper, Kay. *Too Many Rabbits and Other Fingerplays: About Animals, Nature, Weather, and the Universe.* Ill. by Judith Moffatt. New York: Scholastic, 1995.

———, comp. *The Neal-Schuman Index to Fingerplays.* New York: Neal-Schuman, 1993.

Cromwell, Liz, Dixie Hibner, and John R. Faitel. *Finger Frolics Revised.* Ill. by Joan Lockwood. Mt. Rainer, MD: Gryphon House, 1983.

Defty, Jeff. *Creative Fingerplays and Action Rhymes: An Index and Guide to Their Use.* Ill. by author. Phoenix, AZ: Oryx Press, 1992.

Delamar, Gloria T. *Children's Counting-Out Rhymes, Fingerplays, Jump Rope and Bounce-Ball Chants, and Other Rhythms.* Jefferson, NC: McFarland, 1983.

Dowell, Ruth I. *Move Over, Mother Goose! Fingerplays, Action Verses, and Funny Rhymes.* Ill. by Concetta C. Scott. Mt. Rainer, MD: Gryphon House, 1987.

Emerson, Sally. *The Nursery Treasury.* Ill. by Moira Maclean and Colin Maclean. New York: Doubleday, 1988.

Glazer, Tom. *Do Your Ears Hang Low?: Fifty More Musical Fingerplays.* Ill. by Mila Lazarenvich. New York: Doubleday, 1980.

———. *Eye Winker Tom Tinker Chin Chopper: Fifty Musical Fingerplays.* Ill. by Ron Himler. New York: Doubleday, 1973.

Graham, Terry Lynne. *Fingerplays and Rhymes for Always and Sometimes.* Ill. by Linda Eibe and Chip Eibe. Atlanta, GA: Humanics, 1986.

Grayson, Marion. *Let's Do Fingerplays.* Ill. by Nancy Weyl. Washington, DC: Robert B. Luce, 1962.

Hayes, Sarah. *Clap Your Hands.* Ill. by author. New York: Lothrop, Lee & Shepard, 1988.

Hillert, Margaret. *Action Verse for Early Childhood: Fingerplays and Body Movement.* Ill. by author. Minneapolis, MN: T. S. Denison, 1982.

Lamont, Priscilla. *Ring-a-Round-a-Nursery Rhymes, Action Rhymes, and Lullabies.* Ill. by author. Boston: Little, Brown, 1990.

Pooley, Sarah. *A Day of Rhymes.* Ill. by author. New York: Knopf, 1987.

Rogovin, Anne. *Let Me Do It!* Photos by Anne Rogovin and Milton Rogovin. New York: Crowell, 1980.

Totline Staff. *1001 Rhymes and Fingerplays.* Ill. by Gary Mohrmann. Everett, WA: Warren Publishing House, 1994.

Yolen, Jane, ed. *Street Rhymes around the World.* Honesdale, PA: Boyds Mills Press, 1992.

Adelson, Leone. *Who Blew That Whistle?* Ill. by Oscar Fabres. New York: Scott, 1946. 72

Ahlberg, Janet, and Allan Ahlberg. *The Little Worm Book.* Ill. by author. New York: Viking, 1980. 102

Allison, Beverley. *Effie.* Ill. by Barbara Reid. New York: Scholastic, 1990. 4

Anholt, Laurence. *The New Puppy.* Ill. by Catherine Anholt. New York: Artists & Writers Guild, 1995. 74

Appelt, Kathi. *Elephants Aloft.* Ill. by Keith Baker. San Diego: Harcourt Brace Jovanovich, 1993. 50

Armitage, Ronda, and David Armitage. *Ice Cream for Rosie.* Ill. by David Armitage. New York: Dutton, 1981. 52

Armstrong, Jennifer. *That Terrible Baby.* Ill. by Susan Meddaugh. New York: Tambourine Books, 1994. 8

Arnold, Tedd. *Green Wilma.* Ill. by author. New York: Dial, 1993. 48

Arnosky, Jim. *Raccoons and Ripe Corn.* Ill. by author. New York: Lothrop, Lee & Shepard, 1987. 76, 96

Asch, Frank. *Happy Birthday, Moon.* Ill. by author. Englewood Cliffs, NJ: Prentice-Hall, 1982. 62

———. *Mooncake.* Ill. by author. Englewood Cliffs, NJ: Prentice-Hall, 1980. 62

———. *Moondance.* Ill. by author. New York: Scholastic, 1993. 36

———. *Moongame.* Ill. by author. New York: Simon & Schuster, 1984. 62

———. *Oats and Wild Apples.* Ill. by author. New York: Holiday House, 1988. 6

———. *Sand Cake.* Ill. by author. New York: Parents, 1979. 78

———. *Starbaby.* Ill. by author. New York: Scribner's, 1980. 86

———. *Turtle Tale.* Ill. by author. New York: Dial, 1978. 94

Ata, Te. *Baby Rattlesnake.* Ill. by Veg Reisberg. San Francisco: Children's Book Press, 1989. 82

Auch, Mary Jane. *Peeping Beauty.* Ill. by author. New York: Holiday House, 1993. 36

Baker, Alan. *White Rabbit's Color Book.* Ill. by author. New York: Kingfisher Books, 1994. 26

Baker, Keith. *Who Is the Beast?* Ill. by author. San Diego: Harcourt Brace Jovanovich, 1990. 90

Banchek, Linda. *Snake In, Snake Out.* Ill. by Elaine Arnold. New York: Crowell, 1978. 66

Barton, Byron. *Buzz, Buzz, Buzz.* Ill. by author. New York: Macmillan, 1974. 10

Bender, Robert. *A Little Witch Magic.* Ill. by author. New York: Holt, 1992. 100

Benson, Patrick. *Little Penguin.* Ill. by author. New York: Philomel, 1991. 68

Bernhard, Emery. *Ladybug.* Ill. by Durga Bernhard. New York: Holiday House, 1992. 56

Bridwell, Norman. *Clifford's Puppy Days.* Ill. by author. New York: Scholastic, 1994. 74

Brown, Marc. *Arthur's New Puppy.* Ill. by author. Boston: Little, Brown, 1993. 74

Brown, Margaret Wise. *Animals in the Snow.* Ill. by Carol Schwartz. New York: Hyperion, 1995. 84

———. *Goodnight, Moon Pop-Up Book.* Ill. by Clement Hurd. New York: Harper & Row, 1984. 62

Brown, Ruth. *Crazy Charlie.* Ill. by author. Windermer, FL: Rourke, 1982. 2

Burdick, Margaret. *Sara Raccoon and the Secret Place.* Ill. by author. Boston: Little, Brown, 1992. 76

Calhoun, Mary. *Hot-Air Henry.* Ill. by Erick Ingraham. New York: Morrow, 1981. 50

Carle, Eric. *The Grouchy Ladybug.* Ill. by author. New York: Crowell, 1977. 56

———. *The Honeybee and the Robber.* Ill. by author. New York: Philomel, 1981. 10

———. *The Very Hungry Caterpillar.* Ill. by author. New York: Philomel, 1981. 20

———. *The Very Lonely Firefly.* Ill. by author. New York: Philomel, 1995. 46

Carlstrom, Nancy. *Moose in the Garden.* Ill. by

Lisa Desimini. New York: Harper Collins, 1990. 64

Carter, David A. *What's in My Pocket?* Ill. by author. New York: Putnam, 1989. 70

Caseley, Judith. *Grandpa's Garden Lunch.* Ill. by author. New York: Greenwillow, 1990. 96

Cassie, Brian, and Jerry Pallotta. *The Butterfly Alphabet Book.* Ill. by Mark Astrella. Watertown, MA: Charlesbridge Publishing, 1995. 14

Chapman, Cheryl. *Snow on Snow on Snow.* Ill. by Synthia St. James. New York: Dial, 1994. 84

Charles, Oz. *How Is a Crayon Made?* New York: Simon & Schuster, 1988. 34

Chermayeff, Catherine, and Nan Richardson. *Feathery Facts.* Ill. by Ivan Chermayeff. San Diego: Harcourt Brace Jovanovich, 1995. 42

Chlad, Dorothy. *When There Is a Fire Go Outside.* Ill. by author. Chicago: Children's Press, 1982. 44

Chocolate, Debbi. *On the Day I Was Born.* Ill. by Melodye Rosales. New York: Scholastic, 1995. 8

Cousins, Lucy. *What Can Rabbit See?* Ill. by author. New York: Tambourine Books, 1991. 40

Cowcher, Helen. *Antarctica.* Ill. by author. New York: Farrar, Straus & Giroux, 1990. 68

———. *Tigress.* Ill. by author. New York: Farrar, Straus & Giroux, 1991. 90

Craig, Janet. *What's Under the Ocean.* Ill. by Paul Harvey. Mahwah, NJ: Troll, 1982. 78

Cressey, James. *Pet Parrot.* Ill. by Tamasin Cole. Englewood Cliffs, NJ: Prentice-Hall, 1979. 66

Crews, Donald. *Truck.* Ill. by author. New York: Greenwillow, 1980. 18

Day, David. *King of the Woods.* Ill. by Ken Brown. New York: Four Winds Press, 1993. 64

DeGroat, Diane. *Alligator's Toothache.* Ill. by author. New York: Crown, 1977. 2

Delacre, Lulu. *Nathan's Balloon Adventure.* Ill. by author. New York: Scholastic, 1991. 50

Deluise, Dom. *Charlie the Caterpillar.* Ill. by Christopher Santoro. New York: Simon & Schuster, 1990. 20

Demarest, Chris L. *My Little Red Car.* Ill. by author. Honesdale, PA: Boyds Mills Press, 1992. 18

———. *No Peas for Nellie.* Ill. by author. New York: Macmillan, 1988. 96

Demuth, Patricia Brennan. *Max, the Bad-Talking Parrot.* Ill. by Bo Zaunders. New York: Dodd, Mead, 1986. 66

———. *Those Amazing Ants.* Ill. by S. D. Schindler. New York: Macmillan, 1994. 4

DePaola, Tomie. *The Cloud Book.* Ill. by author. New York: Holiday House, 1975. 24

———. *Tony's Bread.* Ill. by author. New York: Putnam, 1989. 12

Dorros, Arthur. *Ant Cities.* Ill. by author. New York: Crowell, 1987. 4

Dubanevich, Arlene. *Calico Cows.* Ill. by author. New York: Viking, 1993. 32

Eastman, P. D. *Sam and the Firefly.* Ill. by author. New York: Random House, 1958. 46

Edwards, Richard. *Moles Can Dance.* Ill. by Caroline Anstey. Cambridge, MA: Candlewick Press, 1994. 60

Ehlert, Lois. *Feathers for Lunch.* Ill. by author. San Diego: Harcourt Brace Jovanovich, 1990. 42

———. *Growing Vegetable Soup.* Ill. by author. San Diego: Harcourt Brace Jovanovich, 1987. 96

———. *Mole's Hill.* Ill. by author. San Diego: Harcourt Brace Jovanovich, 1994. 60

———. *Planting a Rainbow.* Ill. by author. San Diego: Harcourt Brace Jovanovich, 1988. 26

———. *Snowballs.* Ill. by author. San Diego: Harcourt Brace Jovanovich, 1995. 84

Ericcson, Jennifer A. *No Milk!* Ill. by Ora Eitan. New York: Tambourine Books, 1993. 32

Ernst, Lisa Campbell. *A Colorful Adventure of the Bee Who Left Home One Monday Morning and What He Found along the Way.* Ill. by Lee Ernst. New York: Lothrop, Lee & Shepard, 1986. 10

———. *Zinnia and Dot.* Ill. by author. New York: Viking, 1992. 38

Etow, Carole, ill. *Cowboy Pup.* Westport, CT: Wishing Well Books, 1993. 30

———. *Fireman Bear.* Westport, CT: Wishing Well Books, 1993. 44

Faulkner, Keith. *The Wide-Mouthed Frog.* Ill. by Jonathan Lambert. New York: Dial, 1996. 48

Florian, Douglas. *Turtle Day.* Ill. by author. New York: Crowell, 1989. 94

Ford, Miela. *Sunflower.* Ill. by Sally Noll. New York: Greenwillow, 1995. 88

Fowler, Allan. *So That's How the Moon Changes.* Chicago: Children's Press, 1991. 62

Fox, Mem. *Shoes from Grandpa.* Ill. by Patricia Mullins. New York: Watts, 1990. 80

Freeman, Don. *A Pocket for Corduroy.* Ill. by author. New York: Viking, 1978. 70

Freschet, Berniece. *The Ants Go Marching.* Ill. by Stephan Martin. New York: Scribner's, 1973. 4

Gardella, Tricia. *Just Like My Dad.* Ill. by Margot Apple. New York: Harper Collins, 1993. 30

Gelman, Rita Golden. *A Koala Grows Up.* Ill. by Gioia Fiammenghi. New York: Scholastic, 1986. 54

Geoghegan, Adrienne. *Dogs Don't Wear Glasses.* Ill. by author. New York: Crocodile Books, 1996. 40

Giannini, Enzo. *Zorina Ballerina.* Ill. by author. New York: Simon & Schuster, 1993. 36

Gibbons, Gail. *Fire! Fire!* Ill. by author. New York: Harper & Row, 1984. 44

———. *Monarch Butterfly.* Ill. by author. New York: Holiday House, 1989. 14

———. *The Seasons of Arnold's Apple Tree.* Ill. by author. San Diego: Harcourt Brace Jovanovich, 1984. 6

———. *Stargazers.* Ill. by author. New York: Holiday House, 1992. 86

———. *Trucks.* Ill. by author. New York: Crowell, 1981. 18

———. *Whales.* Ill. by author. New York: Holiday House, 1991. 98

Gilliland, Judith Heide. *Not in the House, Newton!* Ill. by Elizabeth Sayles. New York: Clarion, 1995. 34

Gliori, Debi. *Mr. Bear Babysits.* Ill. by author. Racine, WI: Western Publishing, 1994. 8

———. *My Little Brother.* Ill. by author. Cambridge, MA: Candlewick Press, 1992. 8

———. *New Big Sister.* Ill. by author. New York: Bradbury, 1991. 8

Goodenow, Earle. *The Last Camel.* Ill. by author. New York: Walck, 1968. 16

Gordon, Margaret. *Frogs' Holiday.* Ill. by author. New York: Viking, 1986. 48

Gordon, Sharon. *Pete the Parakeet.* Ill. by Paul Harvey. Mahwah, NJ: Troll, 1980. 66

Gravois, Jeanne. *Quickly, Quigley.* Ill. by Alison Hill. New York: Tambourine Books, 1994. 68

Gray, Libba Moore. *Small Green Snake.* Ill. by Holly Meade. New York: Orchard Books, 1994. 82

Griffith, Helen V. *"Mine Will," Said John.* Ill. by Muriel Batherman. New York: Greenwillow, 1980. 74

Grindley, Sally. *Four Black Puppies.* Ill. by Clive Scruton. New York: Lothrop, Lee & Shepard, 1987. 74

Gruber, Suzanne. *Chatty Chipmunk's Nutty Day.* Ill. by Doug Cushman. Mahwah, NJ: Troll, 1985. 22

Haas, Jessie. *Chipmunk!* Ill. by Jos A. Smith. New York: Greenwillow, 1993. 22

Hall, Zoe. *The Apple Pie Tree.* Ill. by Shari Halpern. New York: Blue Sky Press, 1996. 6

Hampshire, Susan. *Rosie's Ballet Slippers.* Ill. by Maria Teresa Meloni. New York: Harper Collins, 1996. 36, 80

Hamsa, Bobbie. *Your Pet Camel.* Ill. by Tom Dunnington. Chicago: Children's Press, 1980. 16

Harrison, David. *When Cows Come Home.* Ill. by Chris L. Demarest. Honesdale, PA: Boyds Mills Press, 1994. 32

Hayes, Sarah. *Bad Egg.* Ill. by Charlotte Voake. Boston: Little, Brown, 1987. 38

Hayles, Karen, and Charles Fuge. *Whale Is Stuck.* Ill. by Charles Fuge. New York: Simon & Schuster, 1993. 98

Heiligman, Deborah. *From Caterpillar to Butterfly.* Ill. by Bari Weissman. New York: Harper Collins, 1996. 14, 20

Henley, Claire. *Joe's Pool.* Ill. by Claire Henley. New York: Hyperion, 1994. 52

Hest, Amy. *Baby Duck and the Bad Eyeglasses.* Ill. by Jill Barton. Cambridge, MA: Candlewick Press, 1996. 40

Hines, Anna Grossnickle. *Moon's Wish.* Ill. by author. New York: Clarion, 1992. 62

———. *Sky All Around.* Ill. by author. New York: Clarion, 1989. 86

Hoff, Syd. *Duncan the Dancing Duck.* Ill. by author. New York: Clarion, 1994. 36.

Hooker, Ruth. *Matthew the Cowboy.* Ill. by Cat Bowman Smith. Niles, IL: Albert Whitman, 1990. 30

Howard, Ellen. *The Big Seed.* Ill. by Lillian

Hoban. New York: Simon & Schuster, 1992. 88

Hubbard, Patricia. *My Crayons Talk.* Ill. by G. Brian Karas. New York: Holt, 1996. 26, 34

Hurd, Thatcher. *Mama Don't Allow.* Ill. by author. New York: Harper & Row, 1984. 2

Hutchins, Pat. *The Doorbell Rang.* Ill. by author. New York: Greenwillow, 1986. 28

———. *Which Witch Is Which?* Ill. by author. New York: Greenwillow, 1989. 100

Imai, Miko. *Little Lumpty.* Ill. by author. Cambridge, MA: Candlewick Press, 1994. 38

Irvine, Georgeanne. *Sydney the Koala.* Photos by Ron Garriso. Chicago: Children's Press, 1982. 54

Jackson, Ellen. *Ants Can't Dance.* Ill. by Frank Remkiewicz. New York: Macmillan, 1991. 4

Jeffrey, Graham. *Thomas the Tortoise.* Ill. by author. New York: Crown, 1988. 94

Jeschke, Susan. *Angela and Bear.* Ill. by author. New York: Holt, 1979. 34

Johnson, Crockett. *Harold and the Purple Crayon.* Ill. by author. New York: Harper, 1955. 34

Johnson, Hannah Lyons. *Let's Bake Bread.* Photos by Daniel Dorn. New York: Lothrop, Lee & Shepard, 1973. 12

Johnston, Tony. *The Witch's Hat.* Ill. by Margot Tomes. New York: Putnam, 1984. 100

Karlin, Nurit. *The Tooth Witch.* Ill. by author. Philadelphia: Lippincott, 1985. 86, 100

Keats, Ezra Jack. *My Dog Is Lost!* Ill. by author. New York: Crowell, 1960. 72

Keller, Holly. *Cromwell's Glasses.* Ill. by author. New York: Greenwillow, 1982. 40

———. *Geraldine's Baby Brother.* Ill. by author. New York: Greenwillow, 1984. 8

Kent, Jack. *The Caterpillar and the Polliwog.* Ill. by author. Englewood Cliffs, NJ: Prentice-Hall, 1982. 20

Kleven, Elisa. *The Lion and the Little Red Bird.* Ill. by author. New York: Dutton, 1992. 26

Kopper, Lisa. *Daisy Thinks She Is a Baby.* Ill. by author. New York: Knopf, 1994. 8, 74

Kraus, Robert. *Owliver.* Ill. by José Arugego and Ariane Dewey. Englewood Cliffs, NJ: Prentice-Hall, 1987. 44

Kroll, Steven. *One Tough Turkey: A Thanksgiving Story.* Ill. by John Wallner. New York: Holiday House, 1982. 92

Kudrna, C. Imbior. *To Bathe a Boa.* Ill. by author. Minneapolis, MN: Carolrhoda, 1986. 82

Kulman, Andrew. *Red Light Stop, Green Light Go.* Ill. by author. New York: Simon & Schuster, 1992. 18

Kunhardt, Edith. *Red Day, Green Day.* Ill. by Marylin Hafner. New York: Greenwillow, 1992. 26

Lesser, Carolyn. *Dig Hole, Soft Mole.* Ill. by Laura Regan. San Diego: Harcourt Brace Jovanovich, 1996. 60

Lester, Helen. *Princess Penelope's Parrot.* Ill. by Lynn Munsinger. Boston: Houghton Mifflin, 1996. 66

Levinson, Riki. *Me Baby!* Ill. by Marylin Hafner. New York: Dutton, 1991. 8

Lindbergh, Reeve. *There's a Cow in the Road.* Ill. by Tracey Campbell Pearson. New York: Dial, 1993. 32

Lindgren, Barbro. *A Worm's Tale.* Ill. by Cecilia Torudd. New York: Farrar, Straus & Giroux, 1988. 102

Lindsey, Treska. *When Batistine Made Bread.* Ill. by author. New York: Macmillan, 1985. 12

Lionni, Leo. *Inch by Inch.* Ill. by author. New York: Astor-Honor, 1960. 102

Lobel, Arnold. *The Rose in My Garden.* Ill. by Anita Lobel. New York: Greenwillow, 1984. 10

London, Jonathan. *Fireflies, Fireflies, Light My Way.* Ill. by Linda Messier. New York: Viking, 1996. 46

———. *Froggy Gets Dressed.* Ill. by Frank Remkiewicz. New York: Viking, 1992. 84

———. *Froggy Learns to Swim.* Ill. by Frank Remkiewicz. New York: Viking, 1995. 48

Loomis, Christine. *One Cow Coughs.* Ill. by author. New York: Ticknor & Fields, 1994. 32

Lorenz, Lee. *Dinah's Egg.* Ill. by author. New York: Simon & Schuster, 1990. 38

Lowery, Linda. *Twist with a Burger, Jitter with a Bug.* Ill. by Pat Dypold. Boston: Houghton Mifflin, 1994. 36

McBratney, Sam. *The Caterpillow Fight.* Ill. by Jill Barton. Cambridge, MA: Candlewick Press, 1996. 20

McCloskey, Robert. *Make Way for Ducklings.* Ill. by author. New York: Viking, 1941. 72

McGuire-Turcatte, Casey A. *How Honu the Turtle Got His Shell*. Ill. by Dick Sakahara. Milwaukee, WI: Raintree, 1991. 94

McKean, Thomas. *Hooray for Grandma Jo!* Ill. by Chris L. Demarest. New York: Crown, 1994. 52

McKee, David. *Elmer in the Snow*. Ill. by author. New York: Lothrop, Lee & Shepard, 1995. 84

McMillan, Bruce. *Going on a Whale Watch*. Photos by author. New York: Scholastic, 1992. 98

———. *Puffins Climb, Penguins Rhyme*. Photos by author. San Diego: Harcourt Brace Jovanovich, 1995. 68

McPhail, David. *Something Special*. Ill. by author. Boston: Little, Brown, 1988. 76

Maestro, Giulio. *Leopard Is Sick*. Ill. by author. New York: Greenwillow, 1978. 58

Mahy, Margaret. *The Horrendous Hullabaloo*. Ill. by Patricia MacCarthy. New York: Viking, 1992. 66

Maris, Ron. *I Wish I Could Fly*. Ill. by author. New York: Greenwillow, 1986. 94

Martin, Bill, Jr. *"Fire! Fire!" Said Mrs. McGuire*. Ill. by Richard Egielski. San Diego: Harcourt Brace Jovanovich, 1996. 44

Mayer, Mercer. *Policeman Critter*. Ill. by author. New York: Simon & Schuster, 1986. 72

———. *There's an Alligator Under My Bed*. Ill. by author. New York: Dial, 1987. 2

Meddaugh, Susan. *The Witches' Supermarket*. Ill. by author. Boston: Houghton Mifflin, 1991. 100

Mogensen, Jan. *The Tiger's Breakfast*. Ill. by author. New York: Crocodile Books, 1991. 90

Mongas, Brian. *Follow That Puppy!* Ill. by R. W. Alley. New York: Simon & Schuster, 1991. 74

Morris, Ann. *Bread Bread Bread*. Photos by Ken Heyman. New York: Lothrop, Lee & Shepard, 1989. 12

Most, Bernard. *Cock-a-Doodle-Moo!* Ill. by author. San Diego: Harcourt Brace Jovanovich, 1996. 32

Newton, Laura P. *William the Vehicle King*. Ill. by Jacqueline Rogers. New York: Bradbury, 1987. 18

Nolan, Dennis. *Witch Bazooza*. Ill. by author.

Englewood Cliffs, NJ: Prentice-Hall, 1979. 100

Numeroff, Laura Joffe. *If You Give a Moose a Muffin*. Ill. by Felicia Bond. New York: Harper Collins, 1991. 64

———. *If You Give a Mouse a Cookie*. Ill. by Felicia Bond. New York: Harper & Row, 1985. 28

O'Connor, Karen. *The Feather Book*. Minneapolis, MN: Dillion Press, 1990. 42

O'Donnell, Elizabeth Lee. *The Twelve Days of Summer*. Ill. by Karen Lee Schmidt. New York: Morrow, 1991. 78

Orbach, Ruth. *Apple Pigs*. Ill. by author. New York: Collins-World, 1977. 6

Parker, Nancy Winslow. *Working Frog*. Ill. by author. New York Greenwillow, 1992. 48

Patrick, Denise Lewis. *Red Dancing Shoes*. Ill. by James E. Ransome. New York: Tambourine Books, 1993. 36

Pelham, David. *Sam's Sandwich*. Ill. by author. New York: Simon & Schuster, 1991. 96

Pene Dubois, William. *Bear Party*. Ill. by author. New York: Viking, 1963. 54

Pete, Bill. *Pamela Camel*. Ill. by author. Boston: Houghton Mifflin, 1984. 16

Pinczes, Elinor J. *One Hundred Hungry Ants*. Ill. by Bonnie MacKain. Boston: Houghton Mifflin, 1993. 4

Polacco, Patricia. *The Bee Tree*. Ill. by author. New York: Philomel, 1993. 10

Polushkin, Maria. *Baby Brother Blues*. Ill. by Ellen Weiss. New York: Bradbury, 1987. 8

Pringle, Laurence. *Twist, Wiggle, and Squirm*. Ill. by Peter Parnall. New York: Crowell, 1973. 102

Radcliffe, Theresa. *The Snow Leopard*. Ill. by John Butler. London, England: Viking, 1994. 58

Raffi. *Baby Beluga*. Ill. by Ashley Wolff. New York: Crown, 1990. 98

Ravilious, Robin. *Two in a Pocket*. Ill. by author. Boston: Little, Brown, 1991. 70

Reiser, Lynn. *The Surprise Family*. Ill. by author. New York: Greenwillow, 1994. 38

Renberg, Dalia Hardof. *Hello, Clouds!* Ill. by Alona Frankel. New York: Harper & Row, 1985. 24

Rey, Margaret. *Curious George Goes to an Ice Cream Shop*. Ill. by author. Boston: Houghton Mifflin, 1989. 52

———. *Curious George Visits a Police Station.* Ill. by author. Boston: Houghton Mifflin, 1987. 72

Richardson, Judith Benet. *Come to My Party.* Ill. by Salley Mavor. New York: Macmillan, 1993. 58

Riddell, Chris. *Bird's New Shoes.* Ill. by author. New York: Holt, 1987. 80

Rivlin, Elizabeth. *Elmo's Little Glowworm.* Ill. by Joe Mathieu. New York: Random House, 1994. 102

Roberts Bethany, and Patricia Hubbell. *Camel Caravan.* Ill. by Cheryl Munro Taylor. New York: Tambourine Books, 1996. 16

Rockwell, Anne. *Apples and Pumpkins.* Ill. by Lizzy Rockwell. New York: Macmillan, 1989. 96

———. *At the Beach.* Ill. by Harlow Rockwell. New York: Macmillan, 1987. 78

———. *Fire Engines.* Ill. by author. New York: Dutton, 1986. 44

Root, Phyllis. *Moon Tiger.* Ill. by Ed Young. New York: Holt, 1985. 90

Rounds, Glen. *Cowboys.* Ill. by author. New York: Holiday House, 1991. 30

Royston, Angela. *Cars.* Photos by Tim Ridley. New York: Macmillan, 1991. 18

Sachar, Louis. *Monkey Soup.* Ill. by Cat Bowman Smith. New York: Knopf, 1992. 34

Schatell, Brian. *Farmer Goff and His Turkey Sam.* Ill. by author. New York: Lippincott, 1982. 92

———. *Sam's No Dummy, Farmer Goff.* Ill. by author. New York: Lippincott, 1984. 92

Seymour, Peter. *What's at the Beach?* Ill. by David A. Carter. New York: Holt, 1985. 78

———. *What's in the Deep Blue Sea?* Ill. by David A. Carter. New York: Holt, 1990. 78

Shaw, Charles G. *It Looked Like Spilt Milk.* Ill. by author. New York: Harper & Row, 1947. 24

Shute, Linda. *How I Named the Baby.* Ill. by author. Morton Grove, IL: Albert Whitman, 1993. 8

Smith, Lane. *Glasses (Who Needs 'Em?)* Ill. by author. New York: Viking, 1991. 40

Snyder, Dick. *One Day at the Zoo.* Photos by author. New York: Scribner's, 1960. 54

Sobol, Harriet Langsam. *A Book of Vegetables.* Photos by Patricia Agre. New York: Dodd, Mead, 1984. 96

Speed, Toby. *Two Cool Cows.* Ill. by Barry Root. New York: Putnam, 1995. 32

Spier, Peter. *Dreams.* Ill. by author. New York: Doubleday, 1986. 24

Spohn, Kate. *Night Goes By.* Ill. by author. New York: Macmillan, 1995. 62, 86

Stadler, John. *The Ballad of Wilbur and the Moose.* Ill. by author. New York: Warner, 1990. 30

Stapler, Sarah. *Spruce the Moose Cuts Loose.* Ill. by author. New York: Putnam, 1992. 64

Stewart, Dianne. *Gift of the Sun: A Tale from South Africa.* Ill. by Jude Daly. New York: Farrar, Straus & Giroux, 1996. 88

Stock, Catherine, *Sophie's Bucket.* Ill. by author. New York: Lothrop, Lee & Shepard, 1985. 78

Stoeke, Janet. *A Hat for Minerva Louise.* Ill. by author. New York: Dutton, 1994. 84

Stone, Kazuko G. *Aligay Saves the Stars.* Ill. by author. New York: Scholastic, 1991. 86

———. *Good Night Twinklegator.* Ill. by author. New York: Scholastic, 1990. 2, 86

Sutherland, Harry A. *Dad's Car Wash.* Ill. by Maxie Chambliss. New York: Atheneum, 1988. 18

Szekeres, Cindy. *Puppy Too Small.* Ill. by author. New York: Golden Books, 1984. 74

Tafuri, Nancy. *Two New Sneakers.* Ill. by author. New York: Greenwillow, 1988. 80

Tate, Lindsey. *Claire and the Friendly Snakes.* Ill. by Jonathan Franklin. New York: Farrar, Straus & Giroux, 1993. 82

Taylor, Kim. *Butterfly.* New York: Dorling Kindersley, 1992. 14

Teague, Mark. *How I Spent My Summer Vacation.* Ill. by author. New York: Crown, 1995. 30

Tokuda, Wendy, and Richard Hall. *Humphrey the Lost Whale.* Ill. by Hanaka Wakiyama. Union City, CA: Heian International, 1992. 98

Tunis, Edwin. *Chipmunks on the Doorstep.* Ill. by author. New York: Crowell, 1971. 22

Turner, Charles. *The Turtle and the Moon.* Ill. by Melissa Bay Mathis. New York: Dutton, 1991. 62, 94

Tusa, Tricia. *Libby's New Glasses.* Ill. by author. New York: Holiday House, 1984. 40

Wagner, Karen. *Chocolate Chip Cookies.* Ill.

by Leah Palmer Priess. New York: Holt, 1990. 28

Wahl, Jan. *Follow Me, Cried Bee!* Ill. by John Wallner. New York: Crown, 1976. 10

Walsh, Ellen Stoll. *Hop Jump.* Ill. by author. San Diego: Harcourt Brace Jovanovich, 1993. 36

———. *Mouse Count.* Ill. by author. San Diego: Harcourt Brace Jovanovich, 1991. 82

———. *Mouse Paint.* Ill. by author. San Diego: Harcourt Brace Jovanovich, 1989. 26

Warren, Cathy. *Victoria's ABC Adventure.* Ill. by Patience Brewster. New York: Lothrop, Lee & Shepard, 1984. 82

Weiss, Leatie. *Funny Feet!* Ill. by Ellen Weiss. New York: Watts, 1978. 68, 80

———. *Heather's Feathers.* Ill. by Ellen Weiss. New York: Watts, 1976. 42

Weller, Frances Ward. *I Wonder If I'll See a Whale.* Ill. by author. New York: Philomel, 1991. 98

Wellington, Monica. *Mr. Cookie Baker.* Ill. by author. New York: Dutton, 1992. 28

Wells, Rosemary. *Abul.* Ill. by author. New York: Dial, 1986. 16

———. *Timothy Goes to School.* Ill. by author. New York: Dial, 1981. 76

West, Colin. *"Buzz, Buzz, Buzz," Went Bumblebee.* Ill. by author. Cambridge, MA: Candlewick Press, 1996. 10

———. *"I Don't Care!" Said the Bear.* Ill. by author. Cambridge, MA: Candlewick Press, 1996. 64

Whitcher, Susan. *Moonfall.* Ill. by Barbara Lehman. New York: Farrar, Straus & Giroux, 1993. 62

Wickstrom, Sylvie K. *Turkey on the Loose!* Ill. by author. New York: Dial, 1990. 92

Wild, Margaret. *All the Better to See You With!* Ill. by Pat Reynolds. Morton Grove, IL: Albert Whitman, 1992. 40

Wilson, Sarah. *Three in a Balloon.* Ill. by author. New York: Scholastic, 1990. 50

Winteringham, Victoria. *Penguin Day.* Ill. by author. New York: Harper & Row, 1982. 68

Wolcott, Patty. *Beware of a Very Hungry Fox.* Ill. by Lucinda McQueen. Reading, MA: Addison-Wesley, 1975. 22

Wong, Herbert H., and Matthew F. Vessel. *My Ladybug.* Ill. by Marie Nonnast Bohlen. Reading, MA: Addison-Wesley, 1969. 56

———. *Our Earthworms.* Ill. by Bill Davis. Reading, MA: Addison-Wesley, 1977. 102

Wright, Kit. *Tigerella.* Ill. by Peter Bailey. New York: Scholastic, 1993. 90

Young, James. *A Million Chameleons.* Ill. by author. Boston: Little, Brown, 1990. 26

Zidrou. *Ms. Blanche, the Spotless Cow.* Ill. by David Merveille. New York: Holt, 1992. 32

Ziefert, Harriet. *Henry's Wrong Turn.* Ill. by author. Boston: Little, Brown, 1989. 98

Title Index

About the Author

Dolores C. Chupela is a children's librarian in Edison, New Jersey. She has won several awards for her publications, including the Middlesex County Citizen-of-the-Week award in celebration of the county's tercentennial.